CRIME, VIOLENCE AND MINORITY YOUTHS

This book is dedicated to my parents,
Mary and L.C. Tatum

A Dream Deferred

What happens to a dream deferred?
Does it dry up
like a raisin in the sun?
Or fester like a sore---
And then run?
Does it stink like rotten meat?
Or crust and sugar over---
like a syrupy sweet?

Maybe it just sags
like a heavy load.

Or does it explode?

-- Langston Hughes, 1951.

Crime, Violence and Minority Youths

BECKY L. TATUM
Georgia State University

Ashgate
Aldershot • Burlington USA • Singapore • Sydney

© Becky L. Tatum 2000

All rights reserved. No part of this publication may be reproduced, stored in a retrieval system or transmitted in any form or by any means, electronic, mechanical, photocopying, recording or otherwise without the prior permission of the publisher.

Published by
Ashgate Publishing Limited
Gower House
Croft Road
Aldershot
Hants GU11 3HR
England

Ashgate Publishing Company
131 Main Street
Burlington, VT 05401-5600 USA

Ashgate website: http://www.ashgate.com

Reprinted 2001

British Library Cataloguing in Publication Data
Tatum, Becky L.
　Crime, violence and minority youths. - (Interdisciplinary research series in ethnic, gender and class relations)
　1. Crime and race - United States 2. Minority youth - United States 3. Juvenile delinquents - United States
　I. Title
　364.3'46'0973

Library of Congress Catalog Card Number: 99-72840

ISBN 1 84014 962 0

Printed and bound in Great Britain by Biddles Limited, Guildford and King's Lynn.

Contents

List of Figures		vi
List of Tables		viii
Preface		x
Acknowledgments		xiii
1	Social Structure and Crime	1
2	Toward a Neocolonial Model	16
3	Colonialism and Mexican Americans	31
4	Developing a Research Agenda	42
5	The Effects of Race and Class	66
6	Pathways to Assimilation and Crime	77
7	Theoretical Promise of the Colonial Perspective	95
References		100
Bibliography		110
Index		113
About the Author		116

List of Figures

1.1	Causal arguments of classic structural perspectives of delinquency and the colonial model	12
2.1	A neocolonial model of adolescent crime and violence	26
6.1	General causal model of delinquency	78
6.2	Causal model using the five measures of alienation and interaction terms based on perceived economic oppression and family support	82
6.3	Causal model using alienation from racial or social group and serious delinquency	83
6.4	Causal model using alienation from the general other and serious delinquency	85
6.5	Causal model using alienation from social praxis and serious delinquency	86
6.6	Causal model using alienation from racial or social group and all measures of delinquency for three racial groups	88-89
6.7	Causal model using alienation from general other and all measures of delinquency for three racial groups	90-91

6.8 Causal model using alienation from social praxis and all
measures of delinquency for three racial groups   92-93

List of Tables

4.1	Comparison of population and sample characteristics	46
4.2	Demographic characteristics of combined sample	48
4.3	Items comprising the perceived oppression scales	54
4.4	Items comprising the alienation scales	56
4.5	Items comprising the delinquency indexes	60
4.6	Incidence of delinquency across the three racial groups	62
5.1	Anova findings for perceived political oppression scale	68
5.2	Anova findings for perceived economic oppression scale	68
5.3	Anova findings for perceived social oppression scale	69
5.4	Anova findings for family support variable	70
5.5	Anova findings for organizational support variable	70
5.6	Anova findings for self-alienation scale	71

5.7	Anova findings for alienation from racial or social group scale	73
5.8	Anova findings for alienation from general other scale	74
5.9	Anova findings for cultural alienation scale	75
5.10	Anova findings for alienation from social praxis scale	75

Preface

Race is a dominant theme in American society. Few issues can be discussed without the factor of race underscoring the analysis. America's obsession with race is rooted in the reality in which the concept is used. Rather than a method of identifying people according to genetic make-up or physical characteristics, race is primarily used to locate and place people according to culturally defined social positions (Rose, 1990). These social positions are unequal and location in the structural hierarchy determines cultural experiences. As a result, it makes a *difference* (emphasis mine) what one is called and into what social position one is placed (Rose, 1990).

Much attention and research have been devoted to the role of race in criminal offending. Crime statistics have traditionally suggested a disproportionate involvement in criminal activity by people of color in comparison to their representation in the population. Official data point to young African Americans, especially young African American males, as being the major perpetrators of crime. From 1980-1990, for example, part one index crime arrests for African American youths ranged from 29% to 37% (FBI, 1991), although they represented less than 5% of the total U.S. population during this time period (Bureau of the Census, 1991). The widest racial gap in juvenile arrests, by far, are for violent crimes, which were reported to be 5 times higher for African American youths than for White youths in 1991 (Snyder and Sickmund, 1993).[1]

Generally, criminologists have attributed high rates of crime and violence among racial minorities to inequities in the social structure. Popular explanations such as social disorganization and strain theories suggest that the greater involvement of nonwhite youths in delinquency is best explained by conditions associated with their lower-class status. These conditions weaken the proficiency of familial and communal institutions to regulate adolescent aspirations and desires, and decrease the ability of nonwhite youths to obtain cultural goals. Blocked opportunities lead to frustration that is acted out through criminal, violent, and delinquent behaviors. The failure of mainstream structural perspectives, however, to explicitly address the role of race and racism in structural relations has lead some minority scholars to suggest the colonial model as an alternative explanation of African American crime and delinquency (Austin, 1983, 1987; Staples, 1975, 1987; Tatum, 1994). From the standpoint of race, the colonial model examines the effects of racial inequality (or oppression) on the personality and behaviors (which are sometimes criminal) of minority individuals. In short, both the mainstream and alternative perspectives argue that crime and delinquency are adaptive responses to structural inequities; the key difference between the two perspectives lies in the use of class versus race as the starting point of analysis.

In *Crime, Violence and Minority Youths*, we critically examine the ability of both classic structural theories and the colonial model to explain high rates of crime among African- and Mexican American youths. We, in turn, propose the neocolonial model as a framework that addresses the limitations of both theoretical perspectives. Findings from a pilot study testing several of the propositions and assumptions of the neocolonial model provide initial insights into the adequacy and theoretical value of the framework.

The contents of the book are presented in seven chapters. Chapter 1 provides a summary of classic structural explanations of delinquency and their limitations in explaining racial differences in adolescent crime. These theories are compared with the colonial model to illustrate how this perspective departs from mainstream theoretical views and what it adds to our understanding of the role of race and racism in criminal and violent behaviors. The theoretical limitations of the colonial model are discussed in Chapter 2. Addressing these limitations, we revise the perspective to form a neocolonial model of adolescent crime and violence.

Although the colonial model is used as a cross-cultural explanation of minority structural experiences, as a theoretical explanation of crime, the perspective has only been applied to African Americans. Chapter 3 examines how structural oppression affects the economic, political and social status of Mexican Americans. Chapter 3 further reviews the Mexican American class structure, in particular, the applicability of the underclass perspective. Finally, the chapter explores how the social structure impacts the structural status of Mexican American youths and the theoretical implications for crime and violence.

In Chapters 4 through 6, the neocolonial model is subjected to empirical analysis. Chapter 4 outlines some methodological issues associated with testing the neocolonial model and describes the characteristics of a pilot study developed to collect initial data. In Chapter 5, we examine if, as posited by the neocolonial model, there are significant differences in levels of perceived oppression, social support, and alienation among African American, Mexican American and White youths. We turn our attention in Chapter 6 to the interrelationships among theoretical variables. A general causal model of delinquency is drawn from the perspective and is tested for the combined sample and by race and types of delinquency.

Finally, in Chapter 7, we provide an overview of the results of the pilot study and offer concluding comments regarding the theoretical promise of the colonial perspective.

Note

[1] Victimization and self-report data suggest similar patterns of juvenile offending (see U.S. Department of Justice, 1992; Huizinga and Elliott, 1987). The National Youth Survey (NYS), however, stresses the importance of distinguishing between prevalence and incidence of delinquency. Prevalence comparisons of delinquent behavior show few differences between African American and White juveniles and youths from lower-, working-, and middle-class backgrounds (Elliott and Ageton, 1980). The incidence of delinquent behavior, however, appears to be greater among low-income and African American juveniles (Elliott and Ageton, 1980).

Acknowledgments

This work is drawn from my dissertation research which examined the utility of the colonial model as a theoretical explanation of minority youth crime. I am deeply indebted to my dissertation committee -- Drs. Terry Thornberry, Frankie Bailey, David Duffee, Alan Lizotte and Graeme Newman -- for their valuable comments and insight during the course of that research project. I am particularly grateful to two individuals: Dr. Terry Thornberry whose profound scholarship in delinquency theory provided the foundation for this research, and to Dr. David Duffee who as Dean of the School of Criminal Justice actively recruited minority students and worked diligently to create an academic environment for them that was both inclusive and receptive to diverse ideologies. I am also indebted to Dr. Ronnie Davis and Dr. Gloria Woods who provided assistance in the collection of data, and the Criminal Justice programs at North Carolina Central University and the University of Illinois at Chicago for their support of my scholarship while I was employed at these institutions. I extend a special thanks to Lois Smith-Owens and the late Dr. Vivian V. Gordon who were invaluable mentors during my course of study at the School of Criminal Justice in Albany. In light of the benefits of the expertise and support of the individuals above, I take full responsibility for the viewpoints expressed in this document as well as any errors and omissions which may have occurred in the completion of this research.

1 Social Structure and Crime

Introduction

The popularity of the social structure perspective as an explanation of lower-class and minority crime is evident from its wide use in criminological research and crime prevention strategies. Generally, theories comprising this paradigm posit that crime is the result of structural inequities in American society. Emphasizing the criminogenic effects of a disadvantaged economic class position, these theories suggest that social factors operating in lower-class areas drive many of its residents into criminal and delinquent behaviors (Einstader and Henry, 1994; Vold, Bernard, and Snipes, 1998).

We begin this chapter with an overview of social disorganization and the Durkheim-inspired strain theories, two of the classic social structure models that have addressed high concentrations of crime among racial and ethnic groups. This discussion is followed by an examination of an alternative view of minority crime, the colonial model, and an assessment of the similarities and differences that exist between the theoretical arguments of the minority and mainstream perspectives.

Structural Theories of Delinquency

Social Disorganization Theory

Social disorganization theory emerged from the ecological research of sociologists at the University of Chicago. The central premise of this theory is that crime and delinquency are linked to the social conditions found in urban environments. Urban areas that are characterized by high levels of poverty, transient populations, and large numbers of incomplete or broken families (to name a few social ills) have social institutions that are ineffective in providing essential services in controlling the behavior of its youths. The breakdown of institutional controls in these areas leads to high rates of delinquency, and over time, the development of a delinquent subculture whose norms and values are transmitted generationally (Einstader and Henry, 1994). In short, the effects of the environment on crime are indirect, operating via social institutions in the community.

The ecological research of Park and Burgess (1925) suggested that the growth of cities followed a pattern of concentric circles that extended from the center of the city outward. Applying the concentric circle theory to delinquency in the city of Chicago, Shaw and McKay (1942, 1969) identified five zones, each with its own structural, organizational and cultural characteristics. Zone I was occupied by commercial headquarters, retail establishments and some commercial recreation. The zone of transition, Zone II, was occupied by the city's poor, unskilled, and disadvantaged, and exhibited the highest levels of social disorganization. Zone III housed the working class while Zones IV and V were the commuter zones of satellite towns and suburbs. Using official records, Shaw and McKay found that delinquency was highest in socially disorganized communities (Zone II) and that this pattern persisted in these areas regardless of the population turnover. More contemporary research has continued to support linkages between the characteristics of inner city neighborhoods (e.g., underclass status, the absence or lack of informal friendship networks and participation in formal organizations) and high official rates of crime and violence among its residents (Sampson and Groves, 1989; Wilson, 1987).

Thus, in explaining minority crime, social disorganization theory emphasizes the characteristics of the communities in which minority youths reside. The theory suggests that: 1) minority youths are more likely to live in disintegrating neighborhoods, and as a result, are associated with social institutions that have lost their ability to regulate aspirations and behavior; and 2) because of residence in these areas, minority youths are less able to achieve the dominant goals of society through conventional means, and therefore, are more likely to turn to crime and delinquency.

Strain Theories

Anomie, opportunity theory, and the theory of delinquent subcultures represent the 'classic' strain theories that have emerged from the Durkheim tradition. Rather than examining community environments, the major focus of these theories is the criminogenic influence of the economic opportunity structure. In his theory of anomie, Merton (1938) argues that all societies have culturally prescribed goals and socially approved means of achieving them. In the United States, individuals aspire to achieve wealth, power, and success which are legitimately obtained through avenues such as education and occupational mobility. The avenues or means of obtaining cultural goals, however, are stratified along class lines. As a result, lower-class youths have fewer legitimate opportunities in which to become structurally successful. The disjunction between cultural goals and structural means to obtain them causes frustration (or strain) that, in turn, leads some lower-class youths to pursue criminal and delinquent means to realize their aspirations. Merton suggests four other adaptations to frustration which include: 1) accepting the cultural goals and institutionalized means of obtaining them (conformity); 2) scaling down or abandoning cultural goals but adhering to institutional means (ritualism); 3) rejecting the cultural goals and institutional means and dropping out of society; and 4) rejecting the cultural goals and institutional means and attempting to create new ones or attempting to make major alterations to the existing social structure (rebellion) (Williams and McShane, 1998: 124-126).

Cohen (1955) and Cloward and Ohlin (1960) both extend the theoretical argument of Merton to examine how limited structural opportunities influence the development of delinquent gang subcultures and the impact on the behavior of lower-class adolescent males (Vold, Bernard and Snipes, 1998).[1] Taking a different view, Cohen characterizes lower-class delinquency as negative and irrational (rather than instrumental) behavior. He specifically argues that delinquent behavior among lower-class youths is actually a protest against middle-class norms and values. Because of their disadvantaged backgrounds, lower-class youths lack the basic skills (e.g., education, communication skills) to compete with their middle-class counterparts. Their inability to gain status and acceptance in conventional society create 'status frustration'-- which Cohen defines as a psychological state involving self-hatred, guilt, self-recrimination, loss of self-esteem and anxiety (Einstadter and Henry, 1994). Lower-class youths react to this frustration in one of three ways. First, they continue to pursue, although unsuccessfully, middle-class values and norms (college boy role). Second, they realize their failure and retreat to the lower-class community (corner boy role). Third, they adopt a set of norms and values in direct opposition to those of the middle-class (a counterculture) and engage in violent and irrational behavior (delinquent boy role).

Cloward and Ohlin (1960) broaden the theoretical argument of anomie theory by examining both the legitimate and illegitimate opportunity structure. These theorists emphasize the fact that opportunities for both conventional and criminal careers may be unavailable to lower-class youths. Cloward and Ohlin argue that although the absence of conventional opportunities may lead to deviant behavior and the formation of delinquent gangs, the type of youth gang that develops is dependent on neighborhood characteristics. Criminal gangs are likely to form in areas where there is an environment for successful criminal enterprises. Communities that are devoid of both conventional and criminal opportunities, on the other hand, are characterized by conflict gangs who express their frustrations through violence. Youths who are unwilling or unable to join criminal or conflict gangs join retreatist gangs who focus on the consumption of drugs and alcohol.

To summarize, strain theories claim that crime and delinquency are the behavioral outcomes of frustration resulting from blocked structural economic opportunities. The higher rates of minority youth offending is associated with their greater concentration in the lower-class, and consequently, more limited access to legitimate avenues in obtaining cultural goals. While the development of delinquent gang subcultures whose behavior is violent and irrational (as suggested by Cohen) is likely, the type of delinquent behavior that is exhibited is also likely to be determined by the illegitimate opportunities that are available to these youths (as suggested by Cloward and Ohlin).

Limitations of Mainstream Explanations

There are four general criticisms of the approach of social disorganization and strain theories to minority youth crime. First, the theoretical models are primarily class-based theories (Einstadter and Henry, 1994; Hirschi,

1969; Williams and McShane, 1998). As noted earlier, these theoretical models assume that high rates of minority youth crime are the result of their lower-class status. This approach confounds the effects of race and class on structural opportunities, frustration (or strain) and social disorganization, and suggests that the impact of the two variables are identical. The importance of analyzing race apart from class is illustrated by Russell who states:

> Examining the impact of relative poverty on criminal offending is not the same as examining the impact of racial inequality on criminal offending. A theoretical analysis that does not recognize this distinction ignores both the pervasiveness of racial inequality and its impact on all Blacks, regardless of class status (1994:310).

Second, mainstream structural theories are ahistorical. In other words, there is no examination of the influence or importance of historical antecedents in determining structural experiences. As a result of the institution of slavery and years of legal discrimination and segregation, the structural experiences of African Americans differ sharply from those of other racial groups (Jaynes and Williams, 1989; Reed, 1993). Yet, mainstream structural models have provided no insight as to the impact of these factors on current structural status or criminal or violent behavior.

Although not only related to minority crime, classic structural models fail to account for differential responses to shared structural conditions. More specifically, the theories do not address why minority youths who face similar situations of structural exclusion choose different behavioral responses.

And fourth, classic structural models measure frustration (or strain) as a global concept. It is quite plausible that youths experience different types of strain[2] and that the various forms of strain will have different effects on crime and delinquency.

The Colonial Model

The colonial model was first proposed as an alternative to traditional theories of race relations, and later as an alternative explanation of Black crime and violence in the works of Austin (1983, 1987)[3] and Staples (1975, 1987). The perspective, which originated with the writings of

Frantz Fanon (1963, 1967), describes how the process of colonialization affects the structural and cultural status of minority individuals. In colonial societies, the economic and political dominance of European Whites enables them to create a social structure in which their culture and values are more salient than those of the minority people. Minority culture is relegated to a lower status, systematically destroyed, and redefined in negative terms. Because of racism, the stratification of minority group members is castelike: members of the dominant group enjoy economic, political and social privileges while minority individuals have little access to society's rewards. Moreover, the primacy of race causes minority individuals of any social class to have lower social status than members of the dominant group. Representatives of the power structure (e.g., soldiers, police) help to maintain this system of superordinate/subordinate relations.

The structural relations in colonial environments affect the personalities of minority individuals. The resulting state of alienation[4] can take five forms. Self-alienation involves feelings of inferiority and self-hatred and disassociation from one's personal identity; it also includes the individual's separation or attempted separation from himself. Alienation from the racial or social group characterizes estrangement from members of one's racial or social group. Estrangement between different racial groups describes alienation from the general other. This form of alienation exemplifies the subordinate/superordinate relationship between minority- and dominant-group members and the violence, paranoia and distrust that exist between the two groups. Cultural alienation includes alienation from one's language and history. Rejecting their native culture, minority individuals adopt the language, culture, and history of the dominant group. Finally, alienation from the social praxis refers to the absence of self-determination, which forms the basis of human potential.

The colonial model suggests three behavioral adaptations to alienation (Bulhan, 1985; Fanon, 1963). First, they may respond to their alienation by assimilating to the dominant culture. This is actually cultural assimilation, whereby minority individuals adopt and/or identify with the major cultural norms and values of the dominant culture. Assimilation to the dominant culture open doors to the limited structural opportunities minority individuals may achieve in the colonial environment (Blauner, 1972).

Second, they may respond to alienation by turning their anger and frustration against themselves and/or other minority individuals. These forms of interpersonal and intrapersonal violence are manifested by high minority crime rates, and particularly by high rates of suicide, homicide, and drug abuse. Fanon does not assume that the targets of minority alienation cannot be members of the dominant culture. Rather, he argues that intragroup violence (e.g., Black on Black) is more likely and is a safer outlet for a continual state of frustration (Fanon, 1967).

Finally, minority individuals may resist the colonial order. This behavioral response involves an attempt to restore traditions and self- and group-confidence. Intragroup violence and other destructive behaviors give way to proactive revolutionary praxis; anger and tensions find appropriate and constructive avenues of expression (Bulhan, 1985:144). In short, protest is a process of decolonization whereby minority individuals attempt to regain control and run their own affairs (Staples, 1987). To achieve this end, Fanon argues that violence against the colonial regime is a necessity (Fanon, 1967).[5]

It is important to note that only one of the three behavioral adaptations is considered to be deviant. Because of its consequences (e.g., the reclaiming of identity), Fanon views revolutionary violence as functional behavior. As with minority individuals, violence is also functional for the dominant group since it is necessary for the creation of the colonial environment and for the maintenance of superordinate/subordinate relations. Dominant group crime and violence used in the creation and maintenance of the colonial order, however, are not labeled as being illegitimate and are not sanctioned. Thus, both labeling and conflict themes underlie the colonial perspective.

Internal Colonialism

Colonialist theorists argue that racial minority groups in the United States are 'internal colonies' that are systemically controlled and exploited by the dominant culture (Blauner, 1972, 1994; Staples, 1975, 1987). These theorists specifically point to the sharp and enduring differentiation in economic, political, and social statuses between minority and majority group members and the economic and political control of minority communities. As in classical colonial societies, the relative permanence of these unequal structural relationships causes alienation (or frustration) among minority individuals that, in turn, may lead to criminal and violent outcomes.

The model of internal colonialism has been widely used to explain the structural relationship of African Americans[6] to dominant society (see Blauner, 1972, 1994; Carmichael and Hamilton, 1967; Clark, 1965; Frazier, 1957; and Staples, 1975, 1987). Taking a historical approach, the model describes the detrimental effects of the institution of slavery and years of discrimination and segregation on current structural status. In the next section, we provide a brief discussion of these structural relations and their potential effects on criminal and violent behavior.

Economic Status

Slavery placed African immigrants at the bottom of the economic, political and social structure.[7] An important source of forced labor in the agricultural South, African slaves represented the lowest and worst of the modern day laborers (Dubois, 1962). Their classification as 'property' and as 'inferior beings' not only precluded their participation in the political system but served as a justification for their subordinate economic and political status.

The lack of economic reform after the institution of slavery was abolished forced most Negro freedmen to enter a system of sharecrop tenant farming in which it was virtually impossible to gain any type of economic independence. Black Codes, which relegated 'persons of color' to the occupation of farmer or servant and allowed police to pick up itinerant African American workers for forced labor, insured a cheap labor supply for plantations (Feagin, 1978; Frazier, 1957; Wilson, 1973).

Outside the agricultural system, African Americans were segregated into 'unskilled Negro jobs', and were prohibited from participating in the expanding industrial sectors in the South. African Americans in northern cities, both prior to and after the Civil War of 1861-1865, faced similar situations, with African American laborers often being displaced by European immigrant workers or forced into lower-level unskilled occupations. Rather than economic promise, the migration of African Americans to the northern urban centers after WWI represented a slow shift from tenant farming and sharecropping to unskilled and semi-skilled jobs in the industrial sector.[8] Thus, the African American worker was denied access to money, jobs and technology that would assure economic advancement within the dominant social structure. Put another way, the racial stratification system in this country placed European laborers above African Americans and afforded them greater opportunities in which to move up the economic ladder.

Colonist theorists argue that these discriminatory employment practices have had long term effects and that the occupational subordination of African Americans can still seen today. African Americans are disproportionately employed in low-wage jobs and goods-producing industries that are particularly sensitive to upward and downward business cycles which affect layoffs and unemployment (Blackwell, 1985; Jaynes and Williams, 1989). Although some of the disparity may be explained by differences in levels of education, part of the disparity can be explained by continuing patterns of discrimination in hiring practices and salaries (Blackwell, 1985; Hacker, 1992). African Americans are often perceived to lack basic skills, work experience or to be less reliable than White workers. Because of these perceptions, some employers recruit through high schools and newspapers that only reach White middle-class neighborhoods (Kirschenman and Neckerman, 1990) or relocate to areas where few African Americans live (Blauner, 1992). Even when African Americans and Whites are matched with similar resumes and trained to behave comparably, research shows that Whites receive about 50% more job offers (Turner, Singleton and Musick, 1991).

Political Status

Internal colonialism further associates the structural subordination of African Americans to their limited political power. Although the period of reconstruction enabled the Negro freedman to experience moderate political participation that resulted in a number of educational and political reforms, this integration was short-lived with their political participation being severely restricted at the end of this period. In the first decade of the twentieth century, the political exclusion of African Americans was directly institutionalized. While European immigrants were able to benefit from urban political machines which played an important role in penetrating discrimination barriers, providing jobs and facilitating upward mobility (Feagin, 1978; Vander Zanden, 1983), the urban political machines were being dismantled by the time African Americans had migrated in large numbers to Northern urban centers. As a result African Americans were not able to fully benefit from the socio-political influence that had been provided to other groups. Furthermore, no other immigrant group faced the degree of systematic exclusion from the urban political system. African Americans were excluded from meaningful participation in White-controlled political machines by practices of gerrymandering and by assignment to positions where the flow of power was unidirectional -- from the party headquarters to the segregated African American institutions. These discriminatory practices prevented them from integrating their interests into the wider politics of the state and nation (Wilson, 1980). Although the second part of the twentieth century shows a dramatic increase in the number of African Americans being elected to local, state and federal offices, which is evidence of increased political power, in comparison to Whites, African Americans have not achieved full participation within the political process (Jaynes and Williams, 1989). And, African American priorities have not been fully appreciated nor are they recognized by either major political party.

Socio-cultural Status

The internal colonialism perspective underscores the importance of the cultural destruction and stigmatization, and the overall lower social status of African Americans. To maximize domination and control, slaves from the same tribes, kingdoms and linguistic groups were separated, a practice that destroyed much of the integral culture of the diverse African people. As a result, when one speaks of the African American culture, he is largely referring to the traditional forms of behaviors, beliefs, values and styles that have grown out of the African American sense of mental and social isolation (Frazier, 1957).[9] While White ethnic groups often gave up their traditional ways in order to assimilate into dominant society, there was no intentional action to destroy their cultural heritage, languages, religions or traits.

African American institutions and cultural practices have traditionally been devalued in dominant society. For example, employers often perceive that diplomas (high school or college) earned at black educational institutions are of "low quality" (Boykin and Ellison, 1994). Black cultural norms such as dress, hair styles and speech are viewed as being appropriate only in the Black community; success and/or acceptance in the dominant structure mean adherence to White cultural norms and the abandonment of Black cultural roots.

Racists' ideologies that have defined African Americans as being biologically inferior underlie their cultural stigmation. While these ideologies are no longer openly proclaimed by community leaders and the laws (e.g., Jim Crow) associated with these ideologies have been abolished, the social status of African Americans for the most part remains lower than the social status of Whites (Feagin and Feagin, 1996; Jaynes and Williams, 1989). The dual stratification system in which African Americans are subjected enables them to obtain status and privileges within the hierarchy of their caste, however, they are not able to alter their group or racial status. Race relegates African Americans to a subordinate status within the larger society.

To summarize, the model of internal colonialism argues that African Americans have suffered greater social, economic and political oppression than their White counterparts. This has been the case historically, and as a consequence of this history, racial inequality between African Americans and Whites is evident today. Structural oppression, however has behavioral consequences. People live within a social context and react to their environment. African Americans are likely to perceive that they are racially oppressed, and as a result of these perceptions, develop feelings of alienation.

Alienation, in turn, leads to assimilation, crime and violence or protest. If crime and violence are the outcome of alienation, the victims are primarily other African Americans. As in the colonial world, it is not uncommon for African Americans to turn their frustration and aggression against themselves or against other African Americans as exhibited in the form of high suicide rates, high rates of drug abuse, and high rates of homicide.

Mainstream vs. Minority Perspective

Although the colonial model is proposed as an alternative to classic structural theories, the two perspectives are noticeably similar (see Figure 1.1). For example, both perspectives posit that individuals in the lower social strata experience blocked structural opportunities that, in turn, lead to frustration that leads to a behavioral response. Crime and violence, which are only one of several possible adaptations, are viewed as normal responses to abnormal social conditions.

Classic Structural Perspectives

Lower Class Status/ ⟶ Limited Structural ⟶ Perception of ⟶ Strain ⟶ Crime
Residence in   Opportunities   Limited Structural
Lower Class   Opportunities
Areas

Colonial Model

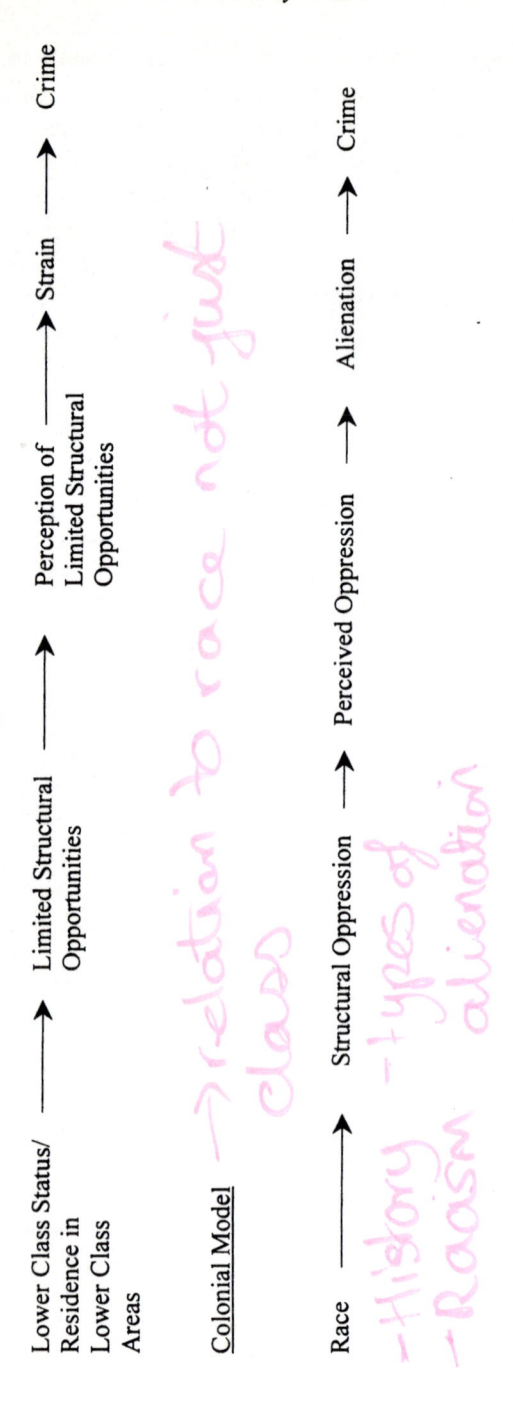

Race ⟶ Structural Oppression ⟶ Perceived Oppression ⟶ Alienation ⟶ Crime

Figure 1.1 Causal arguments of classical structural perspectives of delinquency and the colonial model

Another similarity between the two perspectives is the suggestion that individuals in the lower social strata are cognizant of the limited structural opportunities that are available to them. Last, although the colonial model examines economic, political and social oppression, like classic structural theories, the economic opportunity structure and the inability of certain groups to achieve material success form the basis of both theoretical arguments.

The colonial model, however, moves beyond the classic structural explanations by: 1) explicitly addressing the issue of race and racism; 2) noting the importance of history; and 3) examining types of frustration or alienation. In the colonial model, structural status is primarily measured in terms of race not class. Stated differently, the colonial analysis assesses how society is structured racially and the impact of these racially structured relationships on attitudes and behavior. Also, as opposed to a global measure of strain, the colonial model assesses the role of types of frustrations (or alienation) on crime. Last, the perspective takes into account the role of historical factors, for instance, how a racial group is incorporated into American society, in determining structural experiences.

Summary

In this chapter, we examined how classic structural theories explained minority youth crime, and how these explanations compared to a popular alternative perspective of African American crime, the colonial model. Although there are similarities between the mainstream and alternative perspectives, they differ in important ways--most noticeably, the use of race versus class as the starting point of analysis.

Focusing on class stratification, social disorganization and the Durkheim-inspired strain theories (anomie, opportunity theory and theory of delinquent subcultures) attribute high rates of minority youth crime to: 1) social conditions found in lower class neighborhoods and 2) the limited structural opportunities of lower-class youths to obtain cultural goals. The colonial model argues that the limited structural opportunities that African Americans youths face are primarily the result of race not class. Both explanations suggests that minority youths are cognizant of their social conditions and that frustration arising from these conditions leads to crime and violence. We now turn to examine the adequacy of the theoretical argument proposed by the colonial model.

Notes

1. Cohen and Cloward and Ohlin also drew from the ecological research of Chicago sociologists.
2. Agnew (1992) makes this point in his general strain theory in which he identifies three major types of deviant-producing strain: the failure to achieve an individual's goals, the removal of positive or desired stimuli from the individual, and the confrontation of the individual with negative stimuli.
3. Austin's (1983) macro-level analysis involved Blacks in the Caribbean Island of St. Vincent. Austin examined whether decolonization was accompanied by a decrease in the frequency of intragroup violence.
4. Fanon never defined the concept of alienation. A definition of alienation, however, based on the colonial model can be drawn from the work of Robert Staples. Staples (1987) defines alienation as a feeling of psychological deprivation that arises from the belief that the values of a nation are not congruent with one's own orientation.
5. Austin (1983) also addressed the reaction of mainstream criminologists to Fanon's advocation for revolutionary violence. Austin argues that the prevention of intragroup violence does not require a cathartic letting of blood of the colonizers but merely a sufficient reduction of the impediments to the achievement of conventional values.
6. In this chapter, the terms African American, Black and Negro are used interchangeably.
7. Some of the first Africans who were brought to the American colonies in 1619 were treated as indentured servants. By the mid 1600s, however, the slave status of Africans had been fully institutionalized into the laws of several colonies and was also reflected in the U.S. constitution.
8. A relatively small number of professional African Americans were present; however, because of racism their services were confined to the African American community. Defacto and dejure segregation also restricted these individuals to residences in predominantly African American neighborhoods.

9. There is some disagreement among scholars as to the extent of the destruction of African culture. While Frazier (1957) appears to think that the African culture was virtually destroyed, other scholars suggest that remnants of African culture can still be seen among African Americans today.

2 Toward a Neocolonial Model

Introduction

Despite its attempt to place emphasis on the role of race and racism in minority crime, there are at least three shortcomings in the theoretical logic of the colonial model that limit its explanatory power. First, the perspective does not address the relevancy of experiencing one or several types of alienation. Second, like mainstream explanations, the colonial model does not examine the question of differential responses to shared oppression. Third, the colonial model provides little discussion or insight to the differential class effects of racial oppression, in particular, how structural experiences are presently affected by race and class or how race and class affect attitudes and behaviors. In this chapter, we examine each of these issues and offer a revised perspective for the study of minority youth crime.

Differential Responses to Shared Oppression

Fanon never addressed the question of differential responses to shared oppressive conditions (Bulhan, 1985:198). Throughout his research, however, he described the greater oppressive environment of minority individuals and the absence of effective social, family and community networks. We can infer from this research that person-specific reactions to stress and conflict are a result of personal thresholds that are influenced by social support networks (Fanon, 1967:81). For the purpose of this analysis, we define social support as perceived or actual instrumental and/or expressive provisions supplied by the community, social networks, confiding partners and formal agencies (definition cited by Cullen, 1994).

A sizable amount of literature has examined the interrelationship between social support, stress and mental health. Examining a variety of social contexts and types of support, these studies indicate that social support systems are salient factors in explaining individual reactions to stressful conditions (Anderson, 1991; Gentry and Kobasa, 1984; Myers, 1989), and that these systems often serve as buffers to negative situations (Rook and Dooley, 1982; Spencer, 1995; Smart and Smart, 1995).

A few criminologists have linked the social support concept to crime. According to Cullen (1994), social support is a theme either explicitly or implicitly noted in a large number of mainstream criminological writings. Reviewing both the empirical and theoretical literature, Cullen argues that social support structures (e.g., community, family, formal agencies) are integral factors in reducing criminal involvement and victimization, and are preconditions for effective crime control (1994:545). Agnew (1992) further suggests that conventional social support networks are most effective in reducing criminogenic strain.

Thus, two individuals can suffer from the same sources of political, social and economic exclusion, yet one will assimilate and the other will commit crime or violence. In many cases, this difference in personal thresholds is due to differences in environmental influences such as strong families and social networks that serve as informal sources of support. These factors help the individual to cope with his perceptions of oppression, which in turn, influence his degree of alienation.

Under the same structural conditions, the absence or presence of informal support systems will cause either high or low levels of alienation. The level of alienation influences an individual's behavioral response. Thus an individual's own way of reacting to the environment depends on available informal support.

Therefore, we argue that the difference between those oppressed individuals who commit crimes and those who assimilate is the presence of informal sources of support in the environment. This explanation, however, does not explain why oppressed individuals choose protest as a behavioral response. It is clear that Fanon views protest as a phenomenon separate from assimilation and crime. The type of protest that he describes is a 'radical protest', in which counterviolence is directed against the dominant power who maintains the oppressive social order. As in the case of individuals who respond with assimilation or crime, environmental factors also help these persons to cope with perceived oppression.

Theoretically, those individuals who protest have low levels of alienation from the social praxis (or high self-determination) and low levels of self-alienation, alienation from the racial or social group, and cultural alienation. They also exhibit high levels of alienation from the general other, whom they view as the cause of their oppression. The combination of these factors leads to protest as a behavioral response. Thus for individuals who choose assimilation or protest, the availability of informal social support systems moderates the impact of perceived oppression on alienation, although the types of support varies.

Variants of Alienation

Although the colonial model does not address whether an individual who experiences only one type of alienation is more alienated than one who experiences several types, the model suggests that the five measures of alienation should be empirically related. It also seems reasonable that the more types of alienation an individual experiences, the greater the effect of alienation on behavioral responses.

These premises, however, have not been directly supported by empirical work. Extant studies have used measures of alienation that conceptually differ from those in the colonial model (e.g., powerlessness, normlessness, meaninglessness) or have used a global measure of the concept (see Blackwell and Hart, 1982; Dean, 1961; Moyer and Motta, 1982; Seeman, 1959; Southwell, 1985; Srole, 1956). Despite differences in conceptualization, these measures of alienation have moderate to strong positive correlations (Calabrese, 1989; Blackwell and Hart, 1982; Dean, 1961). Also, at least one study suggests that the more types of alienation that are experienced, the greater the impact on behavior. Southwell (1985) found that individuals who scored highly on three dimensions of alienation (cynicism, powerlessness, and meaninglessness) were less likely to vote than individuals who expressed only one or two of these attitudes. Although these findings have implications for the colonial model, the issue regarding types of alienation can only be resolved through empirical testing of the theoretical model.

Race and Social Class

Discussions about race are incomplete without also talking about class. As noted earlier, the role of class in racial oppression has not been thoroughly examined.[1] It is clear, however, that colonialist theorists view race and class as separate but interacting systems of domination (Feagin and Feagin, 1996). The salience of race and class in American structural stratification, and the contemporary effects of these variables on attitudes and behaviors, can be better understood by integrating aspects of an underclass perspective with the model of internal colonialism.

Underclass theorists agree that historical oppression has impeded African American structural progress. These theorists, however, also suggest that class position and a changing economy contribute to the high rates of violent crime among lower-class African Americans (Anderson, 1990; Wilson, 1987). In particular, underclass theorists point to the deindustrialization of inner cities and the adverse effects of the shift from blue-collar to white-collar, high tech occupations (Bluestone, 1988; Reed, 1993; Wilson, 1987). The decline in the demand for unskilled labor has resulted in the displacement of a significant proportion of the labor force. Because African Americans constitute a disproportionate number of many inner-city populations, and because they are concentrated disproportionately in blue-collar and low-skilled occupations, they have been seriously harmed by these changes in the labor market.

The effect of these economic changes has also varied by class. Middle-class African Americans, who are likely to have the highest levels of education and training, have not suffered as severely from the deindustrialization of the urban centers. In fact, they have been the benefactors of affirmative action programs and the employment and minority contracting opportunities afforded by African American city governments (Boamah-Wiafe, 1990; Jaynes and Williams, 1989; Reed, 1993; Wilson, 1987). These individuals also represent the advancement of African Americans' social status in that lack of employment and educational opportunities have for the most part placed lower-class African Americans largely outside of the American mainstream (Dawson, 1994; Oliver and Shapiro, 1995; Reed, 1993).

Underclass theorists further contrast the structural conditions of lower-class African Americans and Whites. Wilson (1987:58) argues that the communities of poor Whites and poor African Americans differ 'ecologically and economically'. In particular, poor African American communities are more likely to exhibit high rates of unemployment, class segregation, and other social ills. Other researchers have reported similar findings. Jaynes and Williams (1989) find that the poverty rate of African Americans is two to three times higher than that of Whites with similar characteristics. Hacker (1992) notes that fewer than one-quarter of poor Whites who live in urban areas reside in low-income tracts and that some two-thirds of poor whites live in suburban or nonmetropolitan areas. The lower political participation of lower-class African Americans (Hochschild, 1995) combined with their weaker economic base and place of residence also put them at a greater political disadvantage than similarly situated Whites. As a result of these factors, the social status of lower-class African Americans is likely to improve more slowly than that of lower-class Whites (Jaynes and Williams, 1989).

The African American middle-class also lags far behind the White middle-class in regards to economic security, status and wealth (Blauner, 1992; Dawson, 1994; Oliver and Shapiro, 1995; Pettigrew, 1980; Reed, 1993). Middle-class African Americans are employed largely in the public sector and their income is usually based on two working-class wages (Blauner, 1992; Dawson, 1994; Oliver and Shapiro, 1995). Even in professional occupations, African Americans tend to be concentrated in lower-paying, lower-prestige positions. Furthermore, the wealth of middle-class Whites is two and one-half times that of middle-class African Americans (Blauner, 1992). These factors as well as greater susceptibility to economic recessions and governmental budget cuts have resulted in a higher probability that African Americans are less able to transfer their social class status to their children (Oliver and Shapiro, 1995). Although middle-class African-Americans vote, campaign and organize at rates similar to middle-class Whites (Hochschild, 1995), it has not lead to allocational status equal to Whites (Jaynes and Williams, 1989).

We argue that regardless of class, African Americans face situations of structural oppression (Blauner, 1992; Hacker, 1992; Jaynes and Williams, 1989; Oliver and Shapiro, 1995). Race is the master status; it overrides other status considerations. Middle-class status does not protect an African American from being treated first and foremost as an African American (Dawson, 1994; Hacker, 1992). Structural oppression, however, must also be viewed in relation to class status; not all segments of the African American population are equally affected by the economic, political and social structure. Because of their legacy of discrimination, many African Americans are concentrated at the bottom of the structural ladder. These individuals are afflicted sooner, longer and more deeply by negative changes in society, and face the greatest likelihood of remaining outside of the American mainstream (Jaynes and Williams, 1989).

In combination, the underclass model and the model of internal colonialism imply that lower-class African Americans suffer greater structural oppression than either middle-class African Americans or lower-class Whites. Therefore, lower-class African Americans should have the highest levels of perceived oppression. As with middle-class African Americans, informal support systems in the environment will determine whether lower-class African Americans have high or low levels of alienation. The levels of alienation, in turn, will determine their behavioral adaptation.

Racial Inequality and African American Youths

In this section, we describe how race and class influence the structural opportunities (perceived or actual) of African American youths. Decreased demands for unskilled labor and the relocation of industrial jobs have intensified their traditionally higher rates of unemployment and lower rates of labor market participation (Taylor, 1995; Wilson, 1987). Lower-class African American youths, however, have been most adversely affected by these economic changes (Dawson, 1994; Glasgow, 1981). Typically living in the most poverty-stricken inner-city areas, these youths are more likely to be outside the social networks that supply information about or access to jobs. Their social ties are generally other African Americans, who are economically similar to them and who are of little help in providing occupational assistance (Wilson, 1987). White youths, on the other hand, have typically found employment in service sectors rather than in manufacturing (Jaynes and Williams, 1989). Moreover, place of residence and the vertical class structure that characterizes the areas where most poor Whites live also provide the lower-class White youth with more effective social ties and networks that can give information regarding higher-paying positions in the private labor market (Wilson, 1987).

Lack of labor force participation can have prolonged effects on a youth's future employability. In contrast to White teens, increasing numbers of African Americans are entering their twenties without job experience (Dawson, 1994; Reed, 1993). Because they have not been in the labor market, these youths become less employable. Research reveals that employment experience during the high school years significantly improves one's labor market success as a young adult (Sum, Harrington and Goedicke, 1984). Thus lack of job experience can be a permanent handicap for African American youths, especially those who are lower-class (Dawson, 1994).

As suggested above, these changes in the economy have social consequences. Hawkins and Jones (1988) argue that because of more restricted and limited job opportunities, African American youths are more likely to exhibit inappropriate work ethics, low self-esteem, and no sense of future. Hochschild (1995) contends that present economic trends have polarized the African American community. As a result of the migration of middle-class African American families to suburban areas, lower-class African American youths have fewer effective schools and other social institutions that might serve as catalysts for social mobility and social buffers to crime and other social ills (Hochschild, 1995; Wilson, 1987).

Deteriorating economic and social conditions are also likely to affect African American youths' attitudes toward the political structure. Increased African American political representation has failed to improve the structural conditions of most African Americans (Reed, 1993). Because political participation and benefits have been greater for middle-class African Americans and given the different political status of lower-class Whites (Hochschild, 1995), the sense of political powerlessness is arguably more prevalent among lower-class African American youths (Miron and Lauria, 1995).

In summary, the differential impact of the economic, social and political structure on African American teens causes higher levels of perceived oppression for these individuals. Class, however, is an important determinant: lower-class youths face greater structural exclusion than middle-class youth. Due to the interaction effect of race and class, it is the lower-class African American youth who faces the greatest amount of structural exclusion and who has the highest levels of perceived oppression. Whether these perceptions lead to high levels of alienation and crime are dependent upon social support systems in the youth's environment. Social support systems for adolescent populations are discussed in the next section.

Social Support and African American Youths

Family and community and social networks are two important sources of support for adolescent youths. The structure of African American families and its impact on the behavior of its members are a widely debated issue. While some of the living arrangements of African American families have generally been regarded as deviant or pathological because they differ from the family structure of Whites, we are interested in the family forms that have developed and their impact on perceptual, affective, and behavioral adaptations of its members.

According to Stack (1974), a family can be defined as the smallest organized durable network of kin who interacts daily, who provides the domestic needs of children and who assures their survival. Strong families provide at least two mental health functions. First, they provide strong affective support which protects the family and individual family members from external stressors. Second, strong families aid family members in the development of coping strategies to reduce the effects of stressful conditions (Blackwell, 1991; Stack, 1974). In short, the family and their kinship networks provide informal support resources than can affect a youth's level of perceived oppression, influence their level of alienation and indirectly impact their behavioral response. Support exchanges from family and kinship networks can be financial assistance, advice and comfort, goods and services or general help.

Research shows that youths with high parental support are better adjusted (Holahan, Valentiner, and Moss, 1995) and that family and kinship networks are more salient for African Americans because of more limited access to other kinds of social support (Cochran, 1990; Cross, 1990). We argue that because they have greater resources and a smaller probability of structural exclusion, White families on average are more able than African American families to provide their members with informal support. Similarly, middle-class families (African American or White) are more able than lower-class families to provide support to their members. Lower-class African American adolescents are least likely to have this type of informal support. Because of the income and occupational structure, lower-class African American families are less effective than others in performing instrumental (e.g., food, housing, clothing and health care) and affective functions (e.g., feelings of self-worth, social acceptance, and a sense of belonging) (Blackwell, 1991).

Community and social organizations are also important factors in determining whether youths have high or low levels of alienation. We define community and social networks as organizations or institutions in a youth's social environment whose service aid in their socialization and psychological well-being. Youth organizations and programs (e.g., boys' and girls' clubs, sports) are major resources for combating crime, drugs and other problems that threaten adolescents' survival and the quality of life in the community (Billingsley, 1968; Mincy, 1994). Previous research has suggested that participation in social and community organizations is correlated with positive psychological characteristics such as global happiness, self-esteem, and a sense of personal efficacy (Milburn, 1982). Moreover, individuals who are involved in voluntary associations have fewer symptoms of psychological distress than those without such involvement (Gary et al., 1989). These associations often provide adolescents with significant referents who can give advice and the services that can influence the adoption of conventional behaviors (Mincy, 1994).

Quinn (1994) documents wide disparities between upper and lower income communities in the resources available to support youth development. These findings have racial implications. As noted previously, lower-class White youths tend not to reside in low-income areas. Due to the shrinking state and federal resources and the the structural characteristics of neighborhoods, youth organizations and programs in lower-class African American communities are more likely to be associated with the educational systems (1994:123-130). As a result, lower-class African American youths are subjected to fewer program offerings and more limited and less intense program participation.

Many ethnic and racial groups turn to religious behavior and orientation as a reaction to blocked social, economic and political opportunities in the broader society. For these groups, the church has provided a sense of direction, psychological support and coping strategies for dealing with persistent racial prejudice, discrimination and the social stresses of everyday life. African American churches are significant to African American community life in that they represent one of the few indigenous institutions built, controlled and financed by African Americans (Frazier, 1974). The African American church provides many social and organizational functions to the African American community which include: 1) spiritual sustenance as well as a temporary refuge against oppressive conditions that are not found in broader society; 2) serving as outlets for social expression by providing a forum for the discussion of political and social issues and serving as a training ground for potential community leaders; 3) setting guidelines for moral behavior; 4) providing personal aid and support such as advice and encouragement, companionship, goods and services, and financial assistance; 5) encouraging social and educational progress; 6) providing invaluable role models for African American youths by virtue of their involvement in social and/or religious activities; and 7) serving as an agency for the development of African American business structures or ventures (Taylor and Chatters, 1991).[2] Recent research, however, suggests that the role of the African American church as a form of social support for African American adolescents has diminished and is being replaced by government programs and other voluntary organizations (Gibbs, 1990; Rubin, Billingsley, and Caldwell, 1994). The youth programs that are offered tend to be directed toward lower-class youths (Rubin, Billingsley and Caldwell, 1994), which implies that these youths have fewer ties with the African American church or are in more need of this form of social support than their middle-class counterparts.

In sum, family and community and social networks are salient factors in moderating the effects of stressful conditions faced by adolescent youths. However, the availability of these supports vary by race and class. Lower-class African American youths who face the highest levels of structural exclusion are also likely to have the lowest levels of informal social support.

A Revised Perspective

Addressing the limitations of the traditional colonial perspective, we propose a neocolonial model of adolescent crime and violence (see Figure 2.1). According to the causal model, both race and class affect structural oppression. African American teens are subjected to more structural oppression than White teens, and lower-class teens suffer greater amounts of structural oppression than middle-class teens. High amounts of structural oppression result in high levels of perceived oppression. Perceived oppression, however, does not directly influence feelings of alienation. One's degree of alienation depends on the presence or absence of support systems in the environment. Youths whose social environment offers support systems are likely to have low-levels of alienation and thus a

*dashed line means the effect is moderated

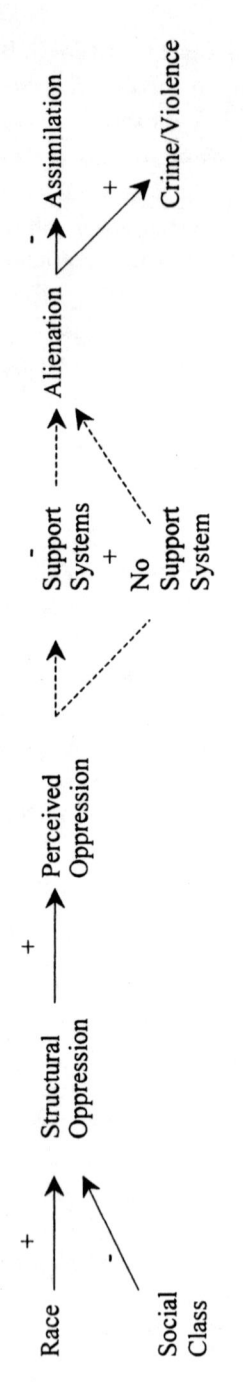

Figure 2.1 A neocolonial model of adolescent crime and violence

higher probability of assimilating to the norms of society. Youths who lack support systems are more inclined to have high levels of alienation, and consequently, to choose delinquency as a behavioral response. On the basis of the causal model, African American youths are likely to have fewer social support systems than White youths, and lower-class youths are likely to have fewer such systems than middle-class youths. The model also suggests an interactive effect between race and class. Lower-class African Americans face the greatest amount of structural exclusion, and are likely to have higher levels of perceived oppression and to lack social support systems than middle-class African Americans and lower-class Whites. Thus, they are most likely to have high levels of alienation and to choose crime and violence as a behavioral response.

Some may argue that youths may place a negative value on assimilation. African Americans have not been able to fully assimilate into the American mainstream. Assimilation may also mean denying one's culture and may weaken group cohesion. Blauner (1994) argues that despite these factors, the vast majority of racial and ethnic minorities in America 'want in'.

Protest is excluded from the model as a behavioral adaptation for adolescents. Although adolescents have previously participated in revolutionary protest movements (e.g., Student Nonviolent Coordinating Committee (SNCC)), there are presently no known student-run organizations advocating counterviolence against the dominant culture (see Carson, 1995). More contemporary acts of adolescent protests or resistance tend to involve student walkouts, sit-ins, physical confrontations with teachers or school administrators or damaging school property. Although these acts are destructive and sometimes involve planning and organization, they are often spontaneous and do not include the organized counterviolence that is described by the neocolonial model.

We can draw five propositions from the neocolonial perspective:

1   Race, social class, and the interaction of these two variables are associated with structural and perceived oppression.
2   Race, social class, and the interaction of these two variables are associated with the availability of social support systems in a youth's environment.

3   Social support systems influence the association between perceived oppression and alienation.
4   Alienation is positively associated with crime and violence.
5   Alienation is inversely associated with assimilation.

Theoretical Contributions

The neocolonial model's contributions to our theoretical understanding of crime and violence among African American youths are threefold. First, unlike the traditional colonial perspective, the neocolonial model provides a better analysis of race and class inequality as both independent and interacting phenomena. The primary argument is that race and class are distinct systems of domination that impact explanatory variables of crime and violence differently. As in the traditional colonial model, racial inequality is the central premise of the revised perspective. Regardless of class, race relegates racial minorities to the lower levels of the stratification system.

Analyzing the interaction effects of race and class permit the examination of important inter- and intragroup differences in structural status and how these differences impact behavioral outcomes. Thus, we are able to assess the effect of class in examining the crimes of middle- and lower-class African American youths; the effects of race in examining the crimes of lower-class White and African American youths; and the effect of race and class in examining the criminality of middle-class White youths and lower-class African American youths. Stated differently, this analysis illustrates the structural inequities that exist within and across racial groups.

Second, as opposed to the more traditional structural models, the neocolonial model is historically grounded. Although the neocolonial model is geared toward contemporary structural status, it examines how this status is affected by past structural experiences. It further assesses how current structural status affects perceptions, attitudes, and behaviors.

Last, as the result of the social support variable and variants of alienation, the theoretical model is able to address issues that have not been resolved in the classic structural theories or the colonial model. More specifically, the perspective is able to assess differences in behavioral outcomes for similarly situated individuals, and the impact of various types of alienation on behavior.

Some may suggest that expanding the argument of the classic structural theories to include a race variable largely negates the relevancy of the alternative explanation. This assumption, however, ignores the difference in theoretical approaches that prevents the simple addition of a race variable. Both the colonial and neocolonial perspective posit that African Americans are colonized people who experience a type of structural domination that differs from that of Whites. Racial colonization results in African Americans regardless of class being afforded fewer structural opportunities than members of the dominant group. Thus, an analysis of the distribution of structural rewards must include an examination of racial privilege and racism in addition to an examination of class position.

Summary

Although the colonial model is proposed as an alternative to classic structural theories, it too falls short in providing an adequate explanation of the high rates of crime among African American youths. In addressing the shortcomings of the colonial model, and at the same time those of classic structural theories, we offer a revised perspective that examines the importance of variants of alienation, differences in individual reactions to stressful conditions, and the interplay between race and class. Empirical analysis of the neocolonial model is presented in Chapters 4, 5 and 6. Before this analysis, we examine the colonial model and its implications for crime for another colonized group, Mexican Americans.

Notes

1   One exception is the work of Mario Barrera (1979) who integrates the internal colonialism perspective with a Marxist definition of social class. Barrera argues that there are four classes in the capitalist U.S.: capitalists, managers, petit bourgeoisie and the working class, each which is crosscut by a line of racial segregation that separates those who suffer from institutional discrimination from those who do not.

2   The same support systems are provided by White churches to members of the White community. The greater degree of structural exclusion that is experienced by African Americans in comparison to Whites, however, makes the African American church a vital component in maintaining cohesion and in ensuring the survival of the African American community.

3 Colonialism and Mexican Americans

Introduction

Hispanic Americans comprise approximately 9% of the American population and are the second largest minority group in the United States (Marger, 1994). The term 'Hispanics', however, is an ethnic label used to refer to several diversified groups who are linked by a shared language and cultural heritage. The three largest Hispanic groups in the United States are Mexican-, Puerto Rican-, and Cuban Americans who collectively comprise 84% of the total Hispanic population.[1]

While most discussions of the colonial perspective involve African Americans, the concept has been applied cross-culturally to describe the structural relationships of Mexican- and Puerto Rican Americans with dominant society (Acuna, 1972; Alvarez, 1973; Blea, 1988; Carr, 1984; Moore, 1970; Murguia, 1975). Both originally entered American society as conquered groups. In comparison, Cuban Americans have primarily come to the United States as voluntary immigrants. Moreover, their immigration, unlike Mexicans or Puerto Ricans, was motivated by political rather than economic factors (Acosta-Belen and Sjostrom, 1988; Feagin, 1978, Marger, 1994). According to the colonial model, these different modes of incorporation, combined with the more adverse socioeconomic experiences that followed, have played a major role in the current structural positions of Mexican- and Puerto Rican Americans in the United States (Acosta-Belen and Sjostrom, 1988; Blea, 1988).

Hispanic Americans hold the ambivalent position of being defined as both a racial and ethnic group. Race (whether they are socially defined as Black or White) plays an important part in the degree of structural inequality that they experience. Racial characteristics among the three major groups of Hispanic Americans, however, vary widely. While the racial background of Mexican Americans is comprised of European and Indian elements, Pureto Ricans have a racial ancestry that primarily consists of European and African descendants. Racially, Cuban Americans are seldom identified as a minority group and because their physical traits are largely indistinguishable from the majority groups (especially the first immigrants), are usually placed in the racial category of 'White' (Bean and Tienda, 1987; Marger, 1994).[2] The salience of race in American society has resulted in greater structural assimilation for Cubans than for their Mexican- and Puerto Rican American counterparts. Puerto Rican Americans are the most disadvantaged group of the three Hispanic groups (Bean and Tienda, 1990; Feagin, 1978; Marger, 1994; Moore and Pinderhughes, 1993).

Sociologist Joan Moore (1970:464) suggests that 'the colonial concept describes and categorizes the Mexican American experience so accurately that one suspects that earlier discovery might have discouraged uncritical application of classical paradigms to all minorities'. This chapter examines historical economic, political and social experiences of Mexican Americans from a colonial perspective. Against this backdrop, we describe the relationship of Mexican American youths with the social structure and the theoretical implications that this relationship has for crime and violence.

Economic Subordination

The subjects of military conquest, the first Mexicans were incorporated into American society at the end of the Mexican War of 1848. Although Mexicans living in the Southwest were promised United States citizenship, they quickly becomes the subjects of a colonial environment. Mexican property was taken through official and unofficial force and fraud, a process that helped transform the group into a colonized work force serving the area's labor needs (Aguirre and Turner, 1995; Feagin, 1978; Marger, 1994). As suggested by Feagin (1978), the dramatic loss of land laid the foundation for the current poverty of many Mexican American communities in that these individuals became landless laborers.

Although the first Mexican citizens represent a case of classical colonialism in which there is forced entry by foreign power and the colonization of a numerical majority, subsequent generations of Mexicans entered the United States as voluntary immigrants in search of economic promise. The colonial conditions that established European dominance over Mexican Americans, however, carried over to the Mexican immigrants who later came to the United States (Feagin and Feagin, 1996). The early economic experiences of people of Mexican descent have included heavy concentration in unskilled and semi-skilled occupations, exclusion from membership in industrial unions, being paid wages for nonwhite workers, and deportation of Mexicans and Mexican Americans when the demand for unskilled labor decreased (Blea, 1988; Feagin and Feagin, 1996). These factors helped to solidify their position in the lower economic ranks.

Occupational data show that Mexican Americans are still primarily concentrated in secondary job markets. The majority of these workers (57%) are service people, production workers and laborers who earn about 63% of the median income of non-Hispanic individuals (Aguirre and Turner, 1995; Bean and Tienda, 1990). In many urban centers, the unemployment rates of Mexican Americans adults and youths parallel those of African Americans (Aguirre and Turner, 1995; Marger, 1994). Because of decreased demands for unskilled and semi-skilled labor and continuing discrimination in employment practices, their economic status is not likely to improve (Martinez, 1996; Turner, Fix, and Struyk, 1991).

Low-levels of educational attainment is also a major factor affecting the economic mobility of Mexican Americans. Mexican Americans have high school dropout rates triple that of Whites and double the rate of African Americans (Feagin and Feagin, 1996). Obu (1991) suggests that Mexican Americans' rejection of public education is a direct reaction to their colonized status in which youths drop out of school to help supplement the family's low income or drop out because of the ethnic discrimination that they face in the school environment.

Political Subordination

Historically, Mexican Americans have held little political power in which to address the adverse structural conditions they faced. From the end of the Mexican American War in 1848 to the 1940s, political participation was limited with few Mexican Americans voting due to fear of Anglo retaliation, apathy or discriminatory political practices (e.g., White primaries, gerrymandering, poll taxes) (Aguirre and Turner, 1995; Blea,

1988; Feagin and Feagin, 1996). Blea (1988:116) notes that the efforts of early Mexican American political organizations such as the Hermanos Penitentes of New Mexico were concentrated in the area of nonelectoral politics.

As a result of political organizations developed by Mexican American veterans, Mexican American's political power increased after World War I. The G.I. Forum and the Community Service Organization advocated: 1) war veteran rights; 2) participation in political elections, particularly elected representation at the local, state and national level; and 3) improved educational opportunities for Mexican American children (Feagin and Feagin, 1996). Political activism among Mexican Americans continued through the 1960s and 1970s with the United Farm Workers (UFW) Union and the more militant Alianza del las Mercedes movement, whose goals were to recover land fraudulently taken from Mexicans in New Mexico (Aguirre and Turner, 1995; Feagin and Feagin, 1996).

In the 1990s, the political participation of Mexican Americans remains in the early stages of development. Their gross underrepresentation at the national, state, and local levels can be directly attributed to the prolonged effects of past discriminatory practices and factors such as language barriers, lower-class status, and immigration. As with African Americans, their political power is limited to those communities and states where they represent the majority. Mexican Americans, however, have not been as effective as African Americans in using political power to address structural issues. It appears that their political participation will continue to lag behind Whites and African Americans for some time to come (Marger, 1994).

Social Subordination

Although Mexican Americans did not endure the levels of discrimination and prejudice experienced by African Americans, they were not treated like European immigrant groups (Aguirre and Turner, 1995; Marger, 1994). In order to rationalize the dispossession of lands and other forms of discrimination, Mexican Americans were stereotyped as being lazy, un-American, backward, immoral and prone to crime and violence. In short, they were not Black, but they also were not White (Feagin, 1978; Marger, 1994). This intermediate status lead to the classification of

Mexicans as a separate racial group, one notch perhaps above Blacks, but clearly inferior to Anglos (Marger, 1994).

Several studies provide support for the intermediate structural status of Mexican Americans. Measuring social distance, Pinkney (1970) found that Whites were more likely to favor integration with Mexican Americans than African Americans. In his book, *Mexican Americans: The Ambivalent Minority*, Skerry (1993) documents various incidents where Mexican Americans were subjected to less discrimination. For example, Mexican American soldiers, unlike soldiers of African American decent, did not fight in segregated units in WWII (1993:295). Other research has shown that residential segregation of African Americans is far greater than Hispanics (as well as other racial groups) regardless of social class status (Jaynes and Williams, 1989). For Hispanics, residential segregation declines as class status increases. However, the degree of residential segregation increases the more similar the Hispanic group is to African Americans in physical appearances (e.g., skin color) (Marger, 1994; Jaynes and Williams, 1989; Massey and Mullen, 1984).

In sum, internal colonialism has involved a variety of groups who are oppressed and exploited in differing degrees and in different fashions. Although their social, economic and political subordination are in many ways similar to African Americans, the structural experiences of Mexican Americans vary in important ways. First, because Mexican Americans never represented a form of forced, unfree labor, the start of their economic status was higher. Second, Mexican Americans never endured a formal system of legalized discrimination (e.g., Black Codes, Jim Crow laws), and in terms of social status, were placed above their African American counterparts. While they exhibit lower levels of political participation and power, economically and socially, Mexican Americans have been afforded more avenues in which to attain the cultural goals of dominant society. As a result of these differences in structural experiences, Mexican Americans' perceptions of economic and social oppression and levels of alienation should be lower than that of African Americans.

The Mexican American Class Structure

Although the underclass perspective is widely used to explain the urban African American class structure, some scholars question the cross-cultural value of the concept.[3] As discussed earlier, the underclass perspective argues that there is a growing polarization between the African American lower- and middle-classes. Middle-class African Americans, who have moved away from the inner cities, have been able to attain some measure of economic, social and political success while the African American lower-class are subjected to high levels of intergenerational poverty, social disorganization, crime and other social ills. Moore and Pinderhughes (1993) contend that while certain elements of the underclass analysis are descriptive of Hispanic neighborhoods, the perspective cannot be applied to this population without modifications.

There is some evidence of a growing Mexican American middle-class. Because of their status and education, middle-class Mexican Americans have been able to adjust to the economic transformation in many urban areas. As a result, they face fewer obstacles to assimilation than working-class Mexican Americans or Mexican immigrants. Acosta-Belen and Sjostrom (1988) note that the oversupply of technical, managerial, and professional personnel in Mexico has resulted in an increase of migrants to the United States who bring with them advanced skills and middle-class cultural orientations. These relatively affluent migrants express alienation from their lower-class counterparts; in fact, the class division between the two groups often results in widely different subcultures (1988:109). For example, it is not uncommon for middle-class Mexican American parents to encourage their children to think of themselves as 'White' and to assimilate to the dominant culture (Feagin and Feagin, 1996).

However, class polarization and single class communities are less characteristic of Mexican Americans. The concentration of poverty in lower-class Mexican American neighborhoods tend not to be the result of the exodus of the middle-class, but rather, other factors such as the influx of poor Mexican immigrants or the economic restructuring of real estate during periods of economic decline and growth (Moore and Pinderhughes, 1993; Rodriguez, 1993; Velez-Ibanez, 1993).[4]

Furthermore, the concentration of poverty in Mexican American neighborhoods does not appear to be as high or as debilitating. In most cities with large Mexican American populations, there are no economically devastated all poor Latinos communities (Padilla, 1983; Velez-Ibanez, 1993). Moreover, these areas tend to exhibit characteristics that both conform and not conform to the definition of an underclass. For instance, Moore and Vigil (1993) in their study of Mexican Americans in Los

Angeles, found widespread poverty, continuing immigration, and strained social institutions in addition to a strong enclave economy, extended families, growing political power, and vital religious organizations. Similarly, Valdez (1993) noted that high levels of economic and social inequality facilitated crime and illegal drug trafficking and drug use in Laredo, Texas; yet this community was also characterized by extended families and residential stability.

Finally, the concentration of poverty in Hispanic communities has positive (as well as negative) effects. Mexican immigrants, who are likely to be poor and to settle in low-income areas, help stimulate enclave economies as a result of their need for low cost housing, and their food, clothing and recreation (Moore and Pinderhughes, 1993). Simply put, for Mexican Americans, the development of underclass conditions and its effects often differ from those in African American communities. Most importantly, these conditions tend to be individual characteristics and do not identify or define a class of people (Moore and Pinderhughes, 1993).

The colonial model can provide some theoretical insight for the variations in urban poverty and its differential effects among African- and Mexican American communities. As noted by Valdez (1993), the more favorable economic and social experiences of Mexican Americans have resulted in communities that are more institutionally complete. This, in addition to the Hispanic culture, serve as buffers to stressful structural conditions. Thus, although the underclass perspective may not describe the structural experiences of Mexican Americans as a group, the combination of the perspective with internal colonialism may be useful in explaining micro-level reactions to structural inequality and how these reactions compare and differ from other minority individuals.

The Social Structure and Mexican American Youths

Most research studies have compared African American youths to White youths, White youths to nonwhite youths or use the collective "Hispanic" label. The literature does suggest, however, that like African American youths, Hispanic youths are also negatively affected by the social structure. Take for example youth unemployment rates. The unemployment rates of Hispanic youths typically fall between those of African American and White youths. Measuring the nature and extent of employment among a national sample of youths age 17-18, Steel (1991) found that weeks of employment statistically differed for White youths (31.77 weeks on average), Hispanic (29.55 weeks) and African American youths (22.57 weeks). As indicated by the data, White youths had the highest levels of employment with the employment levels of Hispanic youths falling between the two groups. The study further noted that Hispanic and African American youths were more likely to be employed in government jobs, which emphasized both groups lack of strong social networks.

Other studies also suggest an intermediate economic status for Hispanic youths. Sum, Harrington and Goedicke (1987) calculated employment/population ratios to determine how well African American, Hispanic and White youths fared in the labor market. The employment/population ratio of African American youths (22.4%) was less than one-half of White youths (46.8%), while the employment/population ratio of Hispanic youths (35.1%) fell between those of African American and White youths. Turner, Fix and Struyk (1991) found that while Hispanics were more likely to be denied equal opportunity for advancement through the hiring process, African Americans were more likely to be denied a job that was offered to a comparable White Anglo applicant. According to Telles and Murguia (1990), unemployment rates and discriminatory employment experiences for Hispanic youths bear close resemblance to African American youths if they are dark-skinned. Examining a specific Hispanic youth subgroup, Bean and Tienda (1990) found that the 1980 unemployment rates of native Mexican American males 16-24 was 13.8% compared to 23.4% for African American males and 11.2% for White males.

Although place of residence plays a salient role in the employability of Hispanic youths, the negative effects of this are less adverse than that experienced by African American youths. Massey and Denton (1993) note that Hispanics are less likely to live in neighborhoods that consist almost entirely of Hispanics, and even when living in areas of extreme poverty, it tends not to be as severe as African Americans. Data comparing Hispanic youths by specific ethnic groups show that 28.2% of Mexican American youths lived in poverty in 1980 compared to 38.6% of African American youths and 11.6% of non-Hispanic White youths (Bean and Tienda, 1987). Because of these factors, Mexican American youths have a higher probability of exposure to a vertical class structure in which there is contact with individuals and families with stable work histories and better social networks in which to gain information or access to jobs.

The higher structural status of Mexican American youths influence their social mobility in other ways. The presence and significance of social support systems in impoverished Mexican American communities was illustrated in our earlier discussion regarding the applicability of the underclass concept to this group. Although structural inequality has lead to high rates of crime and other social ills, the impact of these factors are sometimes buffered by extended families and ethnic economic enclaves found in Hispanic communities. These factors, combined with the greater disparity in racial and class composition of Mexican American neighborhoods result in less structural dislocation for urban Mexican American youths than their African American counterparts.

Theoretical Implications for Crime

Because of the racial categories used to collect crime data (e.g., African American and White, Hispanic and non-Hispanic), our knowledge of crime and violence among Mexican Americans is very limited. The National Crime Victimization Survey in 1992 revealed that the violent crime rate for Hispanic males was 48.5% compared to 37.6% for non-Hispanic males (BJS, 1994). Genelin and Copelin (1989) have estimated that U.S. Latino gangs are responsible for more than one third of all homicides.

Our central question is the role of structural status in the criminal and violent behaviors of Mexican American youths. As discussed in Chapter 1, social disorganization theory suggests that high levels of crime and delinquency are attributable to the characteristics of the communities in which these youths reside. High levels of poverty and employment undermine the ability of social institutions to control criminal and delinquent behavior. Both social disorganization and the strain theories further posit that the structural inequities that these youths face because of class status weakens their ability to achieve the dominant goals of society through conventional means. These youths, as a result, enter into innovative activities in order to obtain structural success.

The neocolonial model analyzes Mexican American youth crime and violence in terms of race and class inequality. Because of the racial hierarchy in American society, Mexican American youths generally have fewer opportunities in which to achieve structural success than White youths. Class stratification presents similar circumstances: lower-class Mexican American youths being afforded fewer structural opportunities than middle-class Mexican American youths. As a result of the interactive effects of both race and class, lower-class Mexican American are more likely to have greater perceptions of oppression, higher levels of alienation and fewer social support systems in which to moderate their frustration in achieving dominant goals. Consequently, lower-class Mexican American youths in comparison to lower-class White youths, and middle-class White and Mexican American youths have a higher probability of engaging in crime and violence.

As a framework of minority crime and violence, the neocolonial model recognizes the variance in the structural experiences of racial minorities and the effects of this variability on attitudes and behavior. The salient differences in the social and economic environments encountered by Mexican Americans should result in these youths having lower levels of perceived economic and social oppression and alienation, and higher levels of social support than African American youths. Lower-class Mexican American youths should exhibit fewer perceptions of perceived economic and social oppression and alienation, and higher levels of social support than lower-class African American youths: middle-class Mexican American youths should exhibit less perceived oppression and alienation, and higher levels of social support than middle-class African American youths. Because of these factors, lower-class African American youths are most likely to participate in criminal and violent behavior.

Summary

This chapter examined the structural experiences of Mexican Americans from an internal colonial perspective. While their relative and absolute social status have improved, they, like African Americans, remain heavily concentrated in the lower economic, social, and political stratums. With the exception of political participation, the economic and social disadvantages of Mexican Americans, however, have not been as adverse or as debilitating as those experienced by African Americans. These differences can possibly account for variations in underclass conditions among lower-class African and Mexican American communities. Although the underclass perspective is not as analogous to the structural conditions of Mexican Americans, we argue that the perspective in combination with internal colonialism may be useful in examining factors that are related to micro-level behavior. According to the neocolonial model, the differential effects of race and class on structural experiences lead to higher levels of structural and perceived oppression, lower levels of social support and higher levels of alienation among African American, and in particular, lower-class African American youths. Thus, lower-class African American youths are the most likely to exhibit high levels of crime and violence with the lowest levels being exhibited by lower-class White youths. For Mexican American youths, levels of structural and perceived oppression, social support, alienation, and crime and violence fall somewhere between those of African Americans and Whites.

Notes

1. According to Aguirre and Turner (1995), Mexican Americans comprise 64% of all Hispanics with Puerto Ricans and Cuban Americans constituting 20%. Twenty-six percent (26%) of the Hispanic population comes from diverse societies in Central and South America.
2. More recent waves of Cubans to the United States mainland are likely to be Black, poor and have criminal records.
3. Wilson (1987) admits that his analysis of urban poverty pertains to inner-city ghettoes in Midwestern and Eastern cities. How much of this analysis can be applied to other regions and localities is debatable.
4. In Houston, Rodriguez (1993) found that during the periods of economic decline apartment landlords engaged in a restructuring strategy to replenish declining middle-income tenants populations with low-income Latino immigrants. When the economy rebounded, rents increased and the housing markets for low-income immigrants shrank.

4 Developing a Research Agenda

Introduction

Few mainstream or alternative perspectives on crime provide insight for testing the theoretical perspective or for measuring key theoretical variables. In this chapter, we attempt to bridge the gap between theory and research by formulating a research agenda for examining the neocolonial model. We begin with a discussion of some key issues that arise in developing a methodological design. Next, we describe the sample, sampling procedures and operationalization of variables for a pilot study used to gather preliminary data to test several of the theoretical assumptions of the perspective.

Testing the Perspective: Some Methodological Issues

At least four methodological issues must be addressed in testing the neocolonial model. The first issue involves the selection of a study sample. While many empirical studies analyzing adolescent crime and violence use samples of in school youths, depending on the nature of the study, these types of samples can pose certain problems. Selecting a sample from a population of in school youths may result in a truncated sample; that is, an analysis of individuals with the most extreme values of the variable(s) under observation. Take for example the key variables that comprise the neocolonial model. Measuring structural and perceived oppression, social support and alienation among in school youths may represent those youths who have the lowest or in the case of social support, highest values for these variables. To get a true sense of how these variables vary among adolescent populations, an ideal sample would include youths from different settings: for example, in school youths, school dropouts, and incarcerated youths. Samples with these characteristics, however, are difficult to collect and are costly. Thus initial tests of the neocolonial model are more likely to involve data collected from a single adolescent subgroup; namely, in school youths.

Voluntary participation is related to the first methodological issue. As with sampling, adolescents who voluntarily participate in research studies may significantly differ from those adolescents who do not participate. The question is: are participants less alienated, have lower levels of perceived oppression and higher levels of social support than nonparticipants?

A third methodological issue is the age of the youths to be studied. Adolescents who are 16 to 18 years of age are arguably better subjects for this type of analysis since it is questionable whether younger adolescents (for example, those 14 years of age) are concerned enough with issues of social, political or economic status. In short, youths age 16-18 youths have a higher probability of being directly affected by the social structure than younger adolescents who tend to largely experience social conditions through parents or other media.

Finally, the measurement of the majority of the variables in the neocolonial model requires the collection of self-report data. Self-report data suffer from a number of limitations which include accurate reporting and lower levels of reliability and validity for minority, male, and lower-class subgroups (Berger, 1995).

A Pilot Study

Pilot studies (or preliminary research conducted under less than perfect conditions) are extremely useful in the initial testing of theoretical perspectives. Because of their exploratory nature, they can illuminate problems regarding the measurement of variables, sampling limitations (and the best way to resolve them), and possible flaws underlying theoretical arguments. Simply put, pilot studies are benchmarks that serve the important function of guiding and helping to assess the feasibility of further analysis. Below we describe the methodology of the pilot study used to collect data to test the theoretical assumptions of the neocolonial model.

Sample and Sampling Procedures

Data for the study are drawn from a survey of two high school populations (separate school districts) in a major Southwestern urban area. The two schools are given the fictitious names of Jefferson and Washington High. Located approximately 25 miles outside of the city limits, Jefferson High School had a student enrollment of 170 juniors and seniors. White students comprised 44% of this population; African- and Mexican Americans students made up 27% and 29% of the population respectively. Located 5 miles outside of the city limits, Washington High School had a student population of 806 juniors and seniors at the time of the study. Racially, 90.6% of the students were African American, 9.2% were Mexican American, and .2% were White. As shown in Table 4.1, the two high school samples did not differ greatly from the populations from which they were drawn.

All students in the populations were asked to voluntarily participate in the study; data from those other than African Americans, Mexican Americans and Whites were later deleted from the analyses. Because of time it would take students to complete the questionnaire (45 minutes), and the schools' concern for instructional time, a mail survey type procedure was used.[1] Survey instruments and parental consent forms were delivered to the principals of each school who gave the items to teachers of junior and senior English and Math courses for distribution.[2] Teachers read survey instructions to students and emphasized that: 1) participation was voluntary; 2) the attached parental consent form had to be signed before the completion of the survey; 3) the survey was to be completed at home in a private setting; and 4) both the survey and the signed parental consent form were to be returned to the principal's office. Only instruments that were returned with signed parental consent forms were accepted by school staff.

The response rate for Jefferson High School was 60%; Washington High School had a response rate of 26%.[3] Based on our observations and the observations and opinions of school officials, it seemed that the requirement of a signed parental consent form greatly affected the return rate for Washington High. We decided to discard the original data for this school and resurveyed the population using passive parental consent. Letters were sent to parent(s) informing them of the nature of the study and the dates for the administration of the survey. If parents did not wish for their child to participate in the study, they were to contact the principal's office before the start of the survey. Students whose parent(s) objected to their child's participation in the study would not be given questionnaires to complete. No student was excluded from the study because their parent(s) refused permission. The response rate for the second data collection effort was 62%.

It is important to note that response rates for mail surveys are typically low and usually do not exceed 50% (Miller, 1991). Although there is no consensus in the survey literature as to what is an acceptable response rate, Babbie (1992) provides the following criteria: 50% is adequate for analysis and reporting; 60% is good; 70% is very good. Based on these standards, the response rates for the two high schools are considered to be good.

Limitations of the Sample

Two criteria for the sample are race and class variability. While the two independent samples have sufficient variability in regards to social class, racial variability is inadequate since Washington High School has few White youths in its student population.

The lack of racial diversity can partially be explained by residential segregation. School districts mirror racial demography. Hacker (1992) indicates that most schools in American are racially segregated. In the state in which this data are drawn, 63.3% of African American children attended segregated schools (1992:163). Segregated schools are especially likely for urban populations. As noted earlier, Washington High School is located five miles outside of the city limits. The number of African Americans and other persons of color increase as one moves towards the inner city. In short, it is unlikely that a large number of White youths will be enrolled in these schools.

Racial stratification as related to residence extends beyond urban areas. In 1980, 86% of suburban Whites still lived in census tracts with less than 1% African American residents (Jaynes and Williams, 1989). This is also reflected by the demographic data of this study which indicate that African American and White youths tend to live in neighborhoods where they are the racial minority (see Table 4.2).

Table 4.1 Comparison of population and sample characteristics

Variable		Jefferson High Population	Jefferson High Sample	Washington High Population	Washington High Sample
Race					
	African American	27% (46)	31% (25)	90.4% (729)	88.4% (410)
	Mexican American	29% (50)	15% (12)	9.2% (74)	11.2% (52)
	White	44% (74)	54% (43)	.2% (2)	.4% (2)
Grade					
	11th	49% (84)	61% (49)	54% (438)	52% (243)
	12th	51% (86)	39% (31)	46% (367)	48% (221)
Gender					
	Male	51% (87)	45% (36)	47% (379)	42% (197)
	Female	49% (83)	55% (44)	53% (426)	58% (267)

Developing a Research Agenda 47

Table 4.1 (continued)

Variable	Jefferson High		Washington High	
	Population	Sample	Population	Sample
Race/Gender				
AA Females	14% (23)	19% (15)	43.1% (347)	37.1% (172)
AA Males	14% (23)	12% (10)	47.4% (382)	51.3% (238)
MA Females	13% (22)	6% (5)	5.2% (42)	5.8% (27)
MA Males	16% (28)	9% (7)	4% (32)	5.4% (25)
White Females	22% (38)	30% (24)	.3% (2)	.4% (2)
White Males	21% (36)	24% (19)	-----[a]	-----[a]

AA=African American; MA=Mexican American
[a]There were no White males in this population and sample

The lack of racial diversity is problematic. If the samples are analyzed separately, Washington High School will not have enough racial variability to make adequate comparisons for White youths. To resolve this problem, the two samples are combined.[4]

Table 4.2 shows that there is in general enough race and class variability for analysis when the samples are combined. The issue, however, is not completely resolved. The combined sample contains only 9 lower-class White youths which prevents any meaningful comparisons with the lower-class youths in the other racial groups. Thus, the data only allow us to test certain theoretical assumptions of the neocolonial model.

We also note that the location of the sample population (the Southwest) does not greatly affect the applicability of the underclass perspective. Although deindustralization is most characteristic of

Table 4.2 Demographic characteristics of combined sample (in percentages)

	African American	Mexican American	White	Total
Race	80 (435)	11.8 (64)	8.2 (45)	100 (544)
Social Class				
Service	42.3 (184)	62.5 (40)	20 (9)	42.8 (233)
Managerial/ Supervisory	45.7 (199)	23.4 (15)	80 (36)	46 (250)
DK/Missing	12 (52)	14.1 (9)	0 (0)	11.2 (61)
Age				
16	33.3 (145)	18.8 (12)	24.4 (11)	30.9 (168)
17	40.7 (177)	46.9 (30)	28.9 (13)	40.4 (220)
18	26 (113)	34.3 (22)	46.7 (21)	28.7 (156)
Mean	16.9	17.2	17.2	17
SD	.77	.72	.82	.77
Grade				
11	53.3 (232)	54.7 (35)	57.8 (26)	53.8 (293)
12	46.7 (203)	45.3 (29)	42.2 (19)	46.1 (251)

Table 4.2 (continued)

	African American	Mexican American	White	Total
Family Structure				
Both parents	63.2 (275)	64 (41)	80 (36)	64.7 (352)
Single mother	32 (139)	29.7 (19)	4.44 (2)	29.4 (160)
Single father	4.8 (21)	6.3 (4)	11.11 (5)	5.5 (30)
Missing	0 (0)	0 (0)	4.44 (2)	.40 (2)
Father's Employment Status				
Employed	73.5 (320)	67.2 (43)	82.2 (37)	73.5 (400)
Unemployed	12.2 (53)	12.5 (8)	8.9 (4)	12 (65)
Missing	14.3 (62)	20.3 (13)	8.9 (4)	14.5 (79)
Mother's Employment Status				
Employed	76.1 (331)	53.1 (34)	68.9 (31)	72.8 (396)
Unemployed	13.6 (59)	34.4 (22)	20 (9)	16.5 (90)
Missing	10.3 (45)	12.5 (8)	11.1 (5)	10.7 (58)

Table 4.2 (continued)

	African American	Mexican American	White	Total
Father's Education				
High school diploma/trade school or less	47.4 (206)	68.8 (44)	33.3 (15)	48.7 (265)
Some college or more	33.3 (145)	10.9 (7)	57.8 (26)	32.7 (178)
Missing	19.3 (84)	20.3 (13)	8.9 (4)	18.6 (101)
Mother's Education				
High school diploma/trade school or less	45.3 (197)	70.3 (45)	35.6 (16)	47.4 (258)
Some college or more	47.6 (207)	20.3 (13)	57.8 (26)	45.2 (246)
Missing	7.1 (31)	9.4 (6)	6.6 (3)	7.4 (40)

Table 4.2 (continued)

Racial Makeup of Residential Neighborhood	African American	Mexican American	White	Total
Predominantly White	5.5 (24)	14.1 (9)	71.1 (32)	12 (65)
Predominantly Black	69.7 (303)	31.3 (20)	0 (0)	59 (323)
Predominantly Hispanic	1.4 (6)	20.3 (13)	0 (0)	4 (19)
Mixed (White, Black, Hispanic)	22.8 (99)	28.1 (18)	17.8 (8)	23 (125)
Other	.20 (1)	3.1 (2)	4.4 (2)	1 (5)
Missing	.40 (2)	3.1 (2)	6.7 (3)	1 (7)

Midwestern urban centers, similar forms of economic restructuring occurred in other regions of the country. For example, from 1983 to 1987, the Southwestern area in this study experienced a period of economic decline in which both African- and Mexican Americans were disproportionately and adversely affected (Valdez, 1993). Although the economy has now improved, it has changed from a primarily industrial economy to a service and high-tech oriented economy.[5]

Unidimensionality and Reliability of Scales

Factor analysis and Cronbach's alpha are used to formulate and to determine the reliability of the scales in the study. Following Smith's (1974) suggestion for scale construction, indicators of the constructs are entered into a principal component analysis with the extraction a single factor. Items that loaded less than .40 on the factor are dropped from the scale.

Although there is no consensus in regards to what constitutes an acceptable reliability coefficient, most researchers agree that alpha coefficients below .60 are unacceptable. This criteria is used as the minimum standard for acceptable alpha levels for scales formulated in this study.

Structural Oppression

The study does not obtain a measure of structural oppression, thus preventing a full test of the neocolonial model. However, we can make theoretical inferences regarding the relationship between structural and perceived oppression. Throughout this study, the link between structural and micro-level behavior is that individuals who are structurally excluded will be cognizant of their exclusion. Theoretically, this premise is illustrated by Cloward and Ohlin's (1960) opportunity theory. Opportunity theory argues that there is an uneven distribution of means in achieving economic success in society and that these means are unequally divided by class position. Specifically, there is the argument that the lower-class is systemically excluded from competitive access to legitimate channels that can lead to economic success. The theory further posits that lower-class youths are goal-oriented individuals who are able to assess their economic situation, and accordingly, plan for the future. In other words, these adolescents perceive that the legitimate opportunity structures are closed. Although they may be exaggerated, these perceptions of exclusion generate behavior. Thus, it is argued that if individuals are structurally oppressed, they will perceive that they are the victims of oppression.

Perceived Oppression Measures

Blauner (1972) defines oppression as the creation and defense of certain privileges for one group over another. Oppression is a type of stratification system in that it creates a bottom rank in a hierarchical system of ranks (Turner, Singleton and Musick, 1990). Because oppression varies by degree, some mobility across ranks is possible. The more complete the denial of material well-being, power and prestige, the greater the oppression (Turner, Singleton and Musick, 1990). A list of the items comprising the perceived oppression scales are provided in Table 4.3.

Perceived political oppression[6] is defined as perceptions that a segment of the population is restricted or denied the type of political participation that can be utilized to achieve levels of material well-being (economic), social prestige, and power that are comparable to other groups. Although there may be limited to moderate political participation by group members, they do not see themselves as being effective in making changes that are beneficial in alleviating the social problems of the group. Some of the items in this scale include: members of my racial group should not bother to vote since none of the candidates will be able to make things better for us and my racial group has more political power than other racial groups. The scale has a Cronbach alpha of .75.

Perceived economic oppression[7] is defined as perceptions that economic opportunities or the state of material well-being are barred from particular groups in society. In short, individuals perceive that access to desirable economic opportunities are based on racial group membership and not on one's skills or qualifications. For example, individuals expressing high levels of perceived economic oppression state that race affects the appearance of financial reliability, place of residence, and educational mobility. The seven item scale has a Cronbach alpha of .62.

The perception that the relative social position of one's racial group is lower than other individuals or groups, and that privileges, statuses or services that are enjoyed by other groups (as a result of their social position) are unavailable to them is the conceptual definition of *perceived*

Table 4.3 Items comprising perceived oppression scales

Perceived political oppression (Alpha =.75)

1. My racial group has more political power than other racial groups.
2. A member of my racial group has a better chance of influencing a political leader than a member of another racial group.
3. My racial group has more influence in our government than other racial groups.
4. Members of my racial group have enough political power to deal with the social problems (e.g., unemployment, poverty, housing and discrimination) that my racial group face.
5. Members of my racial group should not bother to vote since none of the candidates will be able to make things better for us.[a]

Perceived economic oppression (Alpha = .62)

1. People who are educated and who do what is considered proper will be accepted and get ahead.
2. People have only themselves to blame for not doing better in life; if they try harder, they will do better.
3. It's the lack of skills and abilities that keep many people from getting a good job.
4. I can obtain the job I want if I had the proper educational qualifications.
5. All Americans with adequate financial means and with respectable demeanors can choose to live where they wish.
6. If I am hired by an employer, I can be pretty sure it is not because of my race.
7. Whether I use checks, credit cards or cash, I can count on my skin color not to work against my appearance of financial reliability.

Perceived social oppression (Alpha = .68)

1. People like me can choose places to go and not fear that they will be mistreated in these places because of their race.
2. People like me can go shopping most of the time, fairly well assured that they will not be followed or harassed by store detectives.

Table 4.3 (continued)

3	Students of my racial group can easily find classes at school that give attention to the contributions of their race to American civilization.
4	The social status of my racial group is generally viewed as being better than the social status of other racial groups.
5	People of my racial group are widely and positively represented in the newspapers and in television.[a]
6	In American society, people can achieve the social status they want.
7	People like me can do well in challenging situations without being called a 'credit' to their race.
8	If a traffic cop pulls me over, it is not because of my race.

[a]These items are reversed scored so that high scores reflect high levels of perceived oppression.

social oppression.[8] High scorers on this scale state that they cannot find classes at school that give attention to their racial group and that they fear being mistreated in public places. Cronbach alpha for the perceived social oppression scale is .68.

All aspects of oppression in the pilot study are measured as perceptual variables. Items making up each perceived oppression scale use a five point Likert format with high scores indicating high levels of perceived oppression.

Measures of Alienation

Like the perceived oppression subscales, items for each type of alienation also use a five point Likert format with high scores indicating high levels of alienation.[9] Items comprising the alienation scales are provided in Table 4.4.

Table 4.4 Items comprising the alienation scales

Self-alienation (Alpha = .72)

1	I don't like the type of person I am.[a]
2	I feel I do not have much to be proud of.[a]
3	If I was born again, I would prefer to be someone else.[a]
4	There is little or nothing I can do to control what happens to me in life.[a]
5	I don't deserve respect from other people.[a]
6	At times I feel no good at all.[a]

Alienation from the racial or social group (Alpha = .77)

1	For me, home and family never had much positive meaning.[a]
2	Families do not provide security and warmth.[a]
3	Families just restrict a person and give him unnecessary responsibilities.[a]
4	I feel that my family doesn't trust me.[a]
5	I often feel the need to apologize for being a member of my racial group.[a]
6	Anything that members of my racial group do is usually no good.[a]

Alienation from the general other (Alpha = .62)

1	I generally feel that I have a lot of common interests with students of other racial groups at school.
2	People who are members of other racial groups cannot be trusted.[a]
3	People are people regardless of the color of their skin.
4	I get along well with other people.

Cultural alienation (Alpha = .62)

1	The cultural values or beliefs of my racial group should be practiced only where I live and not in wider society.
2	My cultural heritage is inferior to the cultural heritage of other racial groups.

Table 4.4 (continued)

Alienation from the social praxis (Alpha=.72)

1	I can do just about anything I really set my mind to do.
2	I usually expect to succeed in the things I do.

[a]These items are reverse scored so that high scores reflect high levels of alienation.

Self-Alienation is defined as alienation against one's personal identity and has a Cronbach alpha of .72. Some of the questions in this scale include I don't like the type of person I am and I don't deserve respect from other people.

Alienation from the racial or social group identifies estrangement from family, racial or social group members. High scorers on this six item scale express the need to apologize for being a member of their racial group and express embarrassment for the activities of their racial group. The Cronbach alpha for this scale is .77.

Alienation from the general other measures estrangement among different racial groups. Items in this scale ask youths how well they get along with other people, how they view other racial groups, and if they have common interests with students from other racial groups at school. The four items measures alienation has a Cronbach alpha of .62.

Cultural Alienation is defined as estrangement from one's language and history. This two item scale measures perceptions of one's cultural heritage and whether it should be practiced in wider society. It has a Cronbach alpha of .62.

Alienation from the social praxis is measured by two items and is characterized by the abdication of self-determination. With an Cronbach alpha of .72, the subscale assesses whether youths expect to succeed in the thing they do and their degree of perseverance in accomplishing goals.

Social Support Measures

Two variables -- family support systems and organizational support -- are posited to affect whether adolescents assimilate to societal norms or commit criminal or violent acts. Using Stack's (1974) definition, the family is defined as the smallest group of kin who interact daily providing for the domestic needs of children and assuring their survival. Taken from Thornberry, Lizotte, Krohn and Farnworth's (1990) Rochester Youth Developmental Survey, the eight item scale examines how often youths count on family and kin for help, advice and comfort or general support (often=4, sometimes=3, seldom=2 or never=1) in the following areas:

1. Give or loan money to spend?
2. Talk to you about trouble at school?
3. Talk to you about things that are bothering you?
4. Help you in an emergency?
5. Talk to you about problems you are having at home?
6. Talk to you about problems you are having with friends?
7. For advice when you need to make an important decision?
8. To care about you no matter what is happening in your life?

Cronbach alpha for the family support scale is .91.

Organizational support is defined as instrumental or expressive aid that youths receive from adults in community and social organizations. Also taken from the Rochester Youth Development Survey, the six item scale asks youths how often they depend on adults in social and community organization to:

1. To help you in an emergency?
2. To talk to when you are upset?
3. To care about you no matter what is happening in your life?
4. To loan or to borrow money?
5. For advice when you need to make an important decision?
6. To talk about problems you are having at home or school?

The scale has a Cronbach alpha of .98.

Crime Measures

The neocolonial model suggests that adolescents will participate in certain types of criminal behavior. The perception of economic exclusion implies that there will be high rates of property crimes. Adolescents who perceive that they are denied economic opportunities and social status, and that politically their racial group can do little to change this situation may view crime and violence as rational alternatives to achieve desired goals. Since alienated individuals vent their frustration on others or themselves, violent crimes as well as the use of alcohol and drugs (or what the colonial model identifies as intrapersonal violence) also seem likely. Varying levels of perceived oppression, social support, and alienation should result in different levels of participation in these behaviors.

Forty-eight delinquency items from the Rochester Youth Developmental Survey are used to measure crime, violence, and alcohol use (see Table 4.5). These items asked youths how many times they had engaged in the delinquent behaviors during the school year. The items are later categorized into five indexes: serious delinquency, moderate delinquency, minor delinquency, property crimes, and alcohol use. Both the serious and moderate delinquency indexes contain a mixture of violent and property offenses. Although the minor delinquency index does not include offenses that are particularly relevant to the neocolonial model, it is included in the analysis so that the indexes range from serious to minor offenses.

The items in the delinquency indexes are not entered into a factor analysis. Unlike other variables, these items measure behavior that's observable.[10] Because of this, the frequency for each item in an index is summed to yield a total score.[11]

Incidence scores for the five delinquency indexes are presented in Table 4.6. The pattern of the findings suggests that with the exception of serious delinquency, White youths have higher mean levels of offending. Scheffe tests show significant differences in mean scores for moderate delinquency and alcohol use among White youths and African American youths, and White youths and Mexican American youths. Because delinquency scores are skewed toward low values, the scores are presented as natural logs (e.g., ln (frequency of serious delinquency + 1) in subsequent analyses.

Table 4.5 Items comprising the delinquency indexes

Serious delinquency

	1	Stolen or tried to steal a car or other motor vehicle?
	2	Gone into or tried to go into a building to steal or damage something?
	3	Tried to steal or actually stolen money or things between $5 and $50?
	4	Tried to steal or actually stolen money or things over $100?
	5	Attacked someone with a weapon or with the idea of seriously hurting them?
	6	Been involved in a gang fight?
	7	Used a weapon or force to make someone give you money or things?
	8	Physically hurt or threaten to hurt someone to get sex?

Moderate delinquency

	1	Taken someone else's car or motorcycle without permission?
	2	Been drunk in a public place?
	3	Damaged, destroyed, marked up or tagged someone else's property?
	4	Tried to steal or actually stolen money or things worth $5 or less?
	5	Tried to steal or actually stolen money or things between $5 and $50?
	6	Forged a check, used counterfeity money or cashed or used bad checks?
	7	Used or tried to use a credit card, bankcard or automatic teller?
	8	Thrown objects such as rocks or bottles?

Minor delinquency

	1	Been loud or rowdy in a public place?
	2	Tried to steal or actually stolen money or things worth $5 or less?
	3	Run away from home?
	4	Skipped classes without an excuse?
	5	Lied about your age to get into some place?
	6	Hitchhiked a ride with a stranger?

Table 4.5 (continued)

Property crime

1	Damaged, destroyed, marked up or tagged someone else's property?
2	Gone into a building or tried to go into a building to steal or damage something?
3	Tried to steal or have actually stolen money or things $5 or less?
4	Tried to steal or have actually stolen money or things between $5 and $50?
5	Tried to steal or have actually stolen money or things over $100?
6	Tried to buy or sell things that were stolen?
7	Forged a check, used counterfeit money or cashed or used a bad check?
8	Used or tried to use a credit card, bankcard or automatic teller?

Alcohol use

1	Drank beer, wine or wine coolers without your parents' permission?
2	Drank hard liquor without your parents' permission?

Table 4.6 Incidence of delinquency across the three racial groups

Variable Means	African American (N=410)	Mexican American (N=64)	White (N=45)	Total (N=544)
Serious Delinquency	2.10 (5.09)	1.56 (4.83)	2.08 (4.43)	2.03 (5.00)
Moderate[a] Delinquency	3.04 (6.13)	3.14 (5.88)	6.23 (6.76)	3.35 (6.42)
Minor Delinquency	4.02 (6.46)	5.00 (6.52)	6.83 (9.84)	4.36 (6.84)
Property Crimes	2.01 (4.86)	2.16 (4.85)	2.74 (5.11)	2.09 (4.88)
Alcohol[a] Use	5.04 (8.83)	6.34 (6.79)	16.34 (17.48)	6.13 (10.28)

[a] Scheffe tests:
White youths vs. African American youths
White youths vs. Mexican American youths

Standard Deviations are in parentheses

Class

Class is measured by categorizing parents' occupation into service-related (laborers and semi-skilled) and managerial, supervisory or white-collar professions. This neo-Marxist measure of class recognizes the importance of work and labor systems in determining other social forces and relations, and has been used by Farnworth, Thornberry, Krohn and Lizotte (1994) and Hagan, Gillis and Simpson (1985). Households with occupations with parents in both occupational groups are recoded to the occupation with the higher status. We argue that the parent with higher occupational status can provide the benefits that the status brings to the child. Forty-three percent (43%) of the parents are employed in service occupations and 46% are employed in professional, managerial and supervisory positions.

Assimilation[12]

Assimilation is defined as the adoption of the values, attitudes and behaviors of the dominant group. Individuals who assimilate to mainstream society perceive themselves as being similar, if not identical, to dominant group members. This conceptualization also includes the perception that racial characteristics do not serve as foundations for prejudice and discrimination. Assimilation is measured by the following items:

1. I want to see an America -- regardless of race and religion -- that go to the same school.
2. With hard work and perseverance, anyone can achieve the American Dream (e.g., material well-being, social prestige and power).
3. Everyone has a stake in this country. We should all work to help improve it.
4. I think members of minority groups (e.g., African Americans, Hispanic Americans) should wear distinctive hairstyles and clothing.
5. Racial and cultural groups should only form loving relationships and marry within their own racial group.
6. Minorities (e.g., African Americans, Hispanic Americans) should not consider adopting cultural names for themselves.
7. Everyone should try their best to blend into the general American culture.
8. I have difficulty identifying with the American culture.

In order for high scores to reflect high levels of alienation, items 1, 2, 3, 6 and 7 are reversed scored. The scale has a Cronbach alpha of .67.

Summary

This chapter summarized some of the key issues researchers should consider in testing the neocolonial perspective and described the methodology used for a pilot study to collect preliminary data. In Chapter 5, we examine race and class differences in levels of perceived oppression, alienation, and social support. In Chapter 6, we present and test a general causal model of delinquency drawn from the neocolonial model.

Notes

1. School policy did not allow research projects to interfere with instructional time. Thus researchers had two options: to treat the questionnaire as a mail survey as we did in this study or to make arrangements to administer the questionnaire after regular school hours.
2. English and Math are required courses for all juniors and seniors.
3. One hundred and thirty-four surveys were distributed to juniors and seniors at Jefferson High in the first data collection effort; eighty surveys with signed parental consent forms were returned. For Washington High, seven hundred and fifty surveys were distributed; one hundred and ninety-five were returned. In the second data collection effort for Washington High, seven hundred and fifty surveys were distributed and four hundred and sixty-five were returned.
4. The data show few differences among African American and Mexican American youths across school districts.
5. Rodriquez (1995) argues that despite the negative effects of this economic decline, Latino areas did not become socially dislocated communities.
6. Items comprising the perceived political oppression subscale are drawn from Long's (1976) political inefficacy scale plus five additional items constructed by the researcher. Long's (1976) political inefficacy scale has been previously used to assess African American and White adolescents' perceptions of their ability to influence the political system.
7. Items comprising the perceived economic discrimination scale are taken from Long's (1976) economic discrimination scale and McIntosh's (1995) scale of White and male privilege.
8. Several of the items measuring perceived social oppression are drawn from McIntosh's (1995) analysis of White and male privilege.

9   Items comprising the alienation scales are either drawn from the the literature or constructed by the researcher.
10 Menard and Elliott (1994) suggest that delinquency is an observable rather than a latent variable and should not be entered into a factor analysis.
11 As you recall from earlier discussions, the survey was administered at two different points in time. Originally, we asked students at the two high schools to report their involvement in delinquency in September 1992 to May 1993. Because of an initial low response rate, we resurveyed Washington High in September 1993. We asked these students to report their involvement in delinquency from September 1992 to September 1993. As a result, we have one time frame covering a period of nine months and another time frame covering a period of twelve months. We resolved this issue statistically. The incidence scores of youths enrolled at Washington High are first summed and then divided by 12 months. The results of this equation is multiplied by 9 months. Thus, for both schools, the measures refer to the involvement in delinquency over a nine month period. Analysis of the data with and without the adjustment revealed no major changes. The numbers changed slightly but the significance levels remained the same.
12 Items measuring assimilation were drawn from the assimilation literature or were constructed by the researcher.

5 The Effects of Race and Class

Introduction

As noted in Chapter 2, the neocolonial model makes several hypotheses regarding the effects of race and class on perceived oppression and social support. Because of variations in structural exclusion, the perspective argues that the highest levels of perceived oppression (economic and social) and lowest perceptions of social support will be expressed by African American youths followed by Mexican American and White youths. Similarly, lower-class youths are expected to report higher levels of perceived oppression and lower levels of social support than their middle-class counterparts. Interaction effects of race and class are also hypothesized. The interaction effects should show that: 1) lower-class African American youths have the highest levels of perceived oppression and lowest levels of social support followed by lower-class Mexican American and White youths; 2) middle-class African American youths have the highest levels of perceived oppression and lowest levels of social support followed by middle-class Mexican American and White youths; and 3) the highest levels of perceived oppression and lowest levels of social support are exhibited by lower-class African Americans; the lowest levels of perceived oppression and highest levels of social support are exhibited by middle-class White youths.

The neocolonial model assumes that the same variations will be found for the five measures of alienation. Lower levels of social support for African American and lower-class youths should result in higher levels of alienation for these individuals. White youths are expected to have the lowest levels of alienation; levels of alienation for Mexican American youths are expected to fall between those of African American and Whites.

As for interaction effects, lower- and middle-class African American youths should express higher levels of alienation than Mexican American and White youths who are similarly situated. Likewise, levels of alienation for lower- and middle-class Mexican American youths should be lower than African American youths and higher than White youths with the same class status. Finally, the highest levels of alienation should be found among lower-class African-American youths; the lowest levels should be found among middle-class White youths.

This chapter examines the independent and interaction effects of race and class on levels of perceived oppression, social support and alienation for our sample. These analyses are conducted using ANOVA and the Scheffe test of significance.

Perceived Oppression

We begin by examining perceived political oppression. Table 5.1 shows that the measure is not influenced by the independent or interaction effects of race and class.

The small number of lower-class White youths (9) prevents any meaningful interaction analyses involving them in this and subsequent tables. Because of this, interaction effects involving White youths are not noted as being significant in the tables, nor are discussed in the text. Interaction effects among the other racial groups are not significant for the perceived political oppression measure.

There are also no significant race, class or interaction effects for perceived economic oppression (see Table 5.2). As shown in Table 5.3, only significant race effects exist for perceived social oppression. The Scheffe tests reveal that African American youths have higher levels of perceived oppression than both Mexican American and White youths. While these findings are consistent with the theoretical assumptions of the neocolonial model, we do not find significant racial differences in levels of perceived social oppression among Mexican American and White youths.

To summarize, the data offer limited support for race, class and interaction effects on levels of perceived oppression. Hypothesized class and interaction effects are not found. The data do reveal a limited number of significant racial effects that are consistent with hypotheses. As expected, African American youths show higher levels of perceived social oppression than both White and Mexican American youths.

Table 5.1 Anova findings for perceived political oppression scale

	African American	Mexican American	White	Total
Lower Class	10.29 (173)	10.64 (39)	7.22 (9)	10.23 (221)
Middle Class	10.08 (191)	10.80 (15)	9.76 (35)	10.08 (241)
	10.18 (364)	10.69 (54)	9.23 (44)	10.15 (462)

Race   F = 2.96   *ns
Class   F = .00   *ns
Race x Class   F = 3.03   *ns

Table 5.2 Anova findings for perceived economic oppression scale

	African American	Mexican American	White	Total
Lower Class	17.94 (173)	16.56 (39)	18.00 (9)	17.70 (221)
Middle Class	18.18 (191)	17.47 (15)	16.85 (34)	17.95 (240)
	18.06 (364)	16.81 (54)	17.09 (43)	17.83 (461)

Race   F = 2.37   *ns
Class   F = .25   *ns
Race x Class   F = .45   *ns

Table 5.3 Anova findings for perceived social oppression scale

	African American	Hispanic American	White	Total
Lower Class	23.24 (173)	21.95 (39)	20.33 (9)	22.90 (221)
Middle Class	23.37 (191)	22.00 (15)	20.26 (34)	22.84 (240)
	23.31 (364)	21.96 (54)	20.28 (43)	22.87 (461)

Race   F = 7.25 $p < .01$
Class   F = .04   *ns
Race x Class F = .01   *ns

Significant Scheffe Tests:

African American youths vs. White youths
African American youths vs. Mexican American youths

Social Support Systems

Next, we examine the two social support variables, family support and organizational support. As you recall, family support is a global measure that taps youths' perceptions of instrumental and expressive support from family and kin. The organizational support variable examines perceptions of assistance or aid (instrumental and expressive) from adults in social and community organizations. The findings in Tables 5.4 and 5.5 suggest that levels of family and organizational support do not significantly vary by race, class or race and class for our sample.

Table 5.4 Anova findings for family support variable

	African American	Mexican American	White	Total
Lower Class	24.16 (178)	23.87 (38)	21.00 (9)	23.99 (225)
Middle Class	25.16 (191)	24.15 (13)	23.41 (34)	24.86 (238)
	24.68 (369)	23.94 (51)	22.91 (43)	24.43 (463)

Race	$F=2.16$	*ns
Class	$F=3.06$	*ns
Race x Class	$F=.25$	*ns

Table 5.5 Anova findings for organizational support variable

	African American	Mexican American	White	Total
Lower Class	25.96 (178)	27.26 (38)	28.00 (9)	26.26 (225)
Middle Class	24.19 (191)	24.13 (13)	19.53 (34)	23.53 (238)
	25.06 (369)	26.51 (51)	21.30 (43)	24.86 (463)

Race	$F=.98$	*ns
Class	$F=2.73$	*ns
Race x Class	$F=.71$	*ns

Alienation

As noted earlier, race, class, and interaction effects are also posited for the alienation measures. Self-alienation differs significantly for African American and Mexican American youths, but not as anticipated (see Table 5.6). African American youths report lower levels of self-alienation than Mexican American youths. Variations in levels of self-alienation among Mexican American and White youths and among African American and White youths are not observed in the data. Also, the data show no class variations for this variable.

Table 5.6 Anova findings for self-alienation scale

	African American	Mexican American	White	Total
Lower Class	11.49 (177)	14.42 (36)	15.89 (9)	12.14 (222)
Middle Class	11.86 (191)	11.29 (14)	12.40 (35)	11.90 (240)
	11.68 (368)	13.54 (50)	13.11 (44)	11.96 (462)

Race	F=4.95	p < .01
Class	F= .23	*ns
Race x Class	F=4.60	p < .01

Significant Scheffe Tests:
African American vs. Mexican American   p < .01

Significant Interactions:
Lower-class African Americans vs. Lower-class Mexican Americans   p < .05
Middle-class African Americans vs. Lower-class Mexican Americans   p < .05

Significant interactions effects are also found. As indicated by the Scheffe tests, lower-class African American youths have lower levels of self-alienation than Mexican American youths who are similar. This, of course, is opposite to what is suggested by hypotheses. The data further reveal that middle-class African American youths express lower levels of self-alienation than Mexican American youths from lower-class families. The neocolonial model suggests, however, that because of the primacy of race, African American youths regardless of class status will have higher levels of alienation than Mexican American youths.

Although there are no significant race or class effects for alienation from the racial or social group, significant interaction effects do exist. Table 5.7 shows that middle-class African American youths have lower levels of alienation from the racial or social group than lower-class Mexican Americans. Moreover, middle-class Mexican American youths have lower levels of alienation from the racial or social group than lower-class Mexican American youths. Only the second finding is in agreement with expected results.

Racial differences in levels of alienation from the general other (see Table 5.8) are also inconsistent with study hypotheses. White youths report higher mean levels of this type of alienation than both Mexican American and African American youths. Hypotheses suggest, however, that the lowest levels of alienation from the general other should be reported by White youths. Class and interaction effects for this variables are both insignificant. Last, Tables 5.9 and 5.10 reveal no significant race, social class or interaction effects for cultural alienation or alienation from the social praxis.

Table 5.7 Anova findings for alienation from racial or social group scale

	African American	Mexican American	White	Total
Lower Class	11.44 (177)	13.58 (36)	15.56 (9)	11.95 (222)
Middle Class	11.39 (191)	9.98 (14)	11.89 (36)	11.38 (240)
	11.41 (368)	12.50 (50)	12.64 (44)	11.65 (462)

Race   F=2.50   *ns
Class   F=1.95   *ns
Race x Class F=4.35 $p < .01$

Significant Interactions:

Lower-class Mexican Americans vs. Middle-class Mexican Americans $p < .05$
Middle-class African Americans vs. Lower-class Mexican Americans $p < .05$

Table 5.8 Anova findings for alienation from general other scale

	African American	Mexican American	White	Total
Lower Class	7.81 (177)	7.19 (36)	9.33 (9)	7.77 (222)
Middle Class	7.92 (191)	7.21 (14)	8.89 (35)	8.02 (240)
	7.87 (368)	7.20 (50)	8.98 (44)	7.90 (462)

Race   F=4.29 $p < .05$
Class   F= .05   *ns
Race x Class F= .13   *ns

Significant Scheffe Tests:
African American youths vs. White youths $p < .05$
White youths vs. Mexican American youths $p < .05$

Table 5.9 Anova findings for cultural alienation scale

	African American	Mexican American	White	Total
Lower Class	5.12 (177)	4.92 (36)	5.89 (9)	5.12 (222)
Middle Class	5.14 (191)	5.29 (14)	4.40 (35)	5.04 (240)
	5.13 (368)	5.02 (50)	4.70 (44)	5.08 (462)

Race   F= .60   *ns
Class   F= .80   *ns
Race x Class F=2.00   *ns

Table 5.10 Anova findings for alienation from social praxis scale

	African American	Mexican American	White	Total
Lower Class	3.44 (177)	3.83 (36)	4.33 (9)	3.54 (222)
Middle Class	3.21 (191)	3.21 (14)	3.63 (35)	3.27 (240)
	3.32 (368)	3.66 (50)	3.77 (44)	3.40 (462)

Race   F=2.00   *ns
Class   F=2.95   *ns
Race x Class F= .42   *ns

Summary

Do race, social class and the interaction of these variables affect perceived oppression, social support and alienation as posited by the neocolonial model? Overall, limited support is found for theoretical expectations as most of the findings are insignificant. The findings suggest that class is not a factor in the variation of these variables, and race, and the interaction effects only influence certain types of perceived oppression and alienation. Racial differences are found for perceived social oppression, self-alienation and alienation from the general other. The impact of race on the alienation measures are not in the expected direction. African American youths exhibit lower rather than higher levels of self-alienation than Mexican American youths. Also, White youths, who are posited to have the lowest levels of alienation, have the highest levels of alienation from the general other.

Significant interaction effects are limited to self-alienation and alienation from the racial or social group. Across race and class categories, the data suggest that class, not race, is the primary determinant of high or low levels of self-alienation and alienation from the racial or social group. Middle-class African American youths exhibited lower levels of these types of alienation than lower-class Mexican American youths.

In short, it appears that race, class and interaction effects are valid for specific variables and among certain groups. Moreover, none of the significant findings displayed the full range of variations as suggested by the neocolonial model. The findings further point to the complexity of the theoretical perspective and the possibility of other factors impacting hypothesized associations.

6 Pathways to Assimilation and Crime

Introduction

In this chapter, we broaden our analysis to examine the interrelationships among the variables in the neocolonial model. To achieve this end, a general causal model of delinquency is drawn from the perspective and is tested for the combined sample and separately for each racial group.

General Causal Model of Delinquency

The large number of endogenous variables in the neocolonial model (3 perceived oppression variables, 2 social support variables, and 5 alienation variables) makes testing interrelationships somewhat cumbersome. In fact, a test of all interrelationships would involve estimating a total of 30 causal models (3x2x5). Too many models make it difficult to present and analyze the meaning of results.

The causal model we draw from the perspective contains the following variables: race, class, perceived economic oppression, family support, alienation (all measures), assimilation and serious delinquency (see Figure 6.1). We argue that perceived economic oppression is the primary measure of oppression for the neocolonial model. As noted earlier, regardless of how racial minority groups enter a colonial society, the start of their subordination is linked to economic exploitation and incorporation. Economic oppression is suceeded by political and social oppression which are instituted to legitimize and maintain oppressive economic conditions.

Economic status and opportunities affect both the political and

78   *Crime, Violence and Minority Youths*

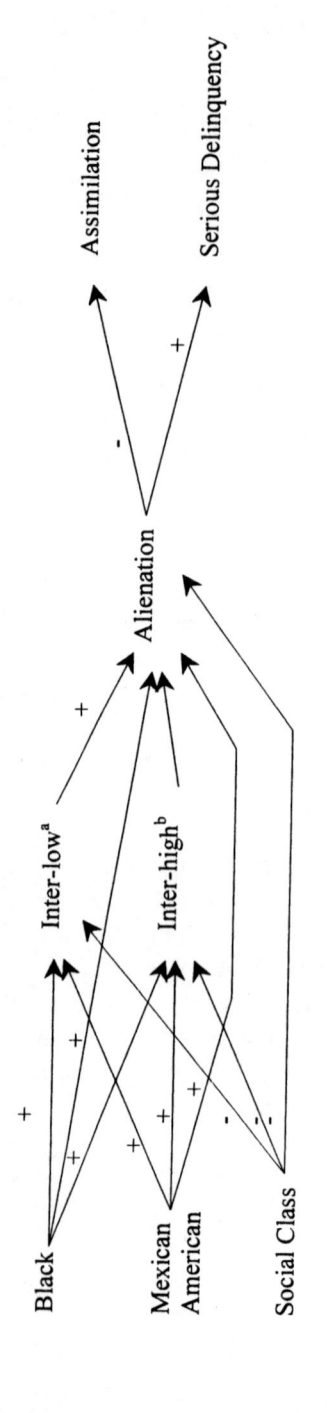

[a] Represents perceived economic oppression and low family support
[b] Represents perceived economic oppression and high family support

Figure 6.1   General causal model of delinquency

social experiences of youths. In *Losing Generations: Adolescents in High-Risk Settings*, the National Research Council (1993) argues that family income is the single most important factor in determining the setting where children and adolescent spend their lives. A family's income and employment status influence housing, neighborhoods, schools and the social opportunities that are linked to them. Simply put, youths who face fewer oppressive economic conditions also tend to face fewer oppressive social conditions. Economics also influence political participation and orientations. Individuals with high social status are not only more likely to vote, but are also more likely to exhibit political efficacy (Jaynes and Williams, 1989). Thus, although perceived social and political oppression are important components of the neocolonial model, perceived economic oppression is arguably the central measure of perceived oppression.

We further posit that family support is the most central social support variable in moderating perceptions of oppression for youths age 16-18. It is the family rather than adults in social and community organizations who is likely to be the most influential in communicating norms and values, modeling appropriate behavior and attitudes, and providing the necessary information about the environment.

Several studies have examined the role of the family in the psychosocial development of youths. Curry (1976) found that familial networks are most influential in the occupation and educational plans of urban adolescents, especially African American youths. Hendin (1987) and Spaights and Simpson (1986) described the African American family as a moderating structure that has traditionally tempered the anger and frustration of African American youths. Examining the role of the family in the etiology of African American adolescent suicide, Hendin (1987) reported that a high degree of alienation from the family was a major causal factor.

Similar studies have indicated the importance of the family for Hispanic populations. High familism among Mexican Americans has been associated with caretaking and financial assistance, lower perceptions of helplessness, and fewer emotional problems (Vernon and Roberts, 1985). Both Rodriquez and Weisburn (1991) and Sommers, Fagan and Baskin (1994) found that the family was a salient variable in moderating Puerto Rican male delinquency.

As you recall, the neocolonial model examines the absence or presence of social support among adolescents. Because no youth reported an absence of social support, the effects of high and low levels of family support are examined. Based on the median of the family support variable, two variables -- high and low family support -- are created. The low family support variable represent values below the median of the original family support measure; the high family support variable represents those values falling above the median. We hypothesize that a positive association will exist between perceived economic oppression and alienation for youth with low levels of family support compared to an inverse association between the variables for youths with high levels of social support. Perceived economic oppression and family support are depicted as two interaction terms that are developed by multiplying the two variables. The first interaction term (inter-low) measures perceived oppression and low levels of family support; perceived oppression and high levels of family support are measured by the second interaction term (inter-high).

The causal model addresses four issues. First, it examines the hypothesized relationships between race, class, perceived oppression and social support. As indicated by the model, race and class are expected to directly affect the interaction terms. Theoretically, perceptions of economic oppression are more prevalent among African Americans and Mexican American youths with low levels of family support than White youths who are similarly situated. The same racial variability is anticipated among youths who have high levels of family support, with African American and Mexican American youths expressing higher levels of perceived oppression than White youths. As for class, lower-class youths with high and low family support are more likely to have perceptions of oppression than their middle-class counterparts.

Second, the causal model examines race and class differences in levels of alienation. As implied by the neocolonial model, African American, Mexican American and lower-class youths should have higher levels of alienation than White or middle-class youths. In short, race and class are expected to have both an indirect (via the interaction terms) and direct effect on the alienation variable.

Third, the causal model addresses whether the effect of perceived oppression on alienation is moderated by social support. Perceived oppression is expected to have a positive effect on levels of alienation for youth with low levels of family support. Thus, the path from inter-low to alienation is expected to be positive. The opposite is anticipated for youths with high levels of family support. For these youths, the path from inter-high alienation should be inverse. Finally, the causal model addresses whether alienation is inversely associated with assimilation and positively associated with delinquency.

Estimation of the Causal Model

The model is estimated five times each time using a different measure of alienation. The results of the equations are not entirely consistent with theoretical explanations. As shown in Figure 6.2, class does not affect the interaction terms or the individual measures of alienation. The race effects approach statistical significance (+$p < .10$). The general pattern of the findings across the five models suggest that: a) African American and Mexican American youths with high levels of family support have greater perceptions of economic oppression than White youths; b) White youths with low levels of family support report greater perceptions of economic oppression than both African- and Mexican American youths; and c) White youths report higher levels of alienation from the general other and lower levels of self-determination than African American youths. The direction of the last two results (b and c) contradict theoretical expectations.

One of the most salient findings is the effects of the interaction terms on the alienation variables. There are no significant interaction effects on self- and cultural alienation. Only one of the two interaction effects (inter-low) on alienation from the racial or social group is significant. The interaction effects on the alienation terms for the model using alienation from the general other and alienation from the social praxis approach statistical significance (+$p < .10$) and are positive. All measures of alienation are positively associated with serious delinquency and inversely associated with assimilation.

Race and Types of Delinquency

Up to this point, we have estimated the causal model using the entire sample and using serious delinquency as the sole measure of delinquent behavior. To assess whether the interrelationships among the variables vary across the three racial groups, we re-estimate the causal model using the variants of alienation with significant interaction effects or interaction effects that approached statistical significance. As shown in Figure 6.3, the model using alienation from the racial or social group is fairly inconsistent

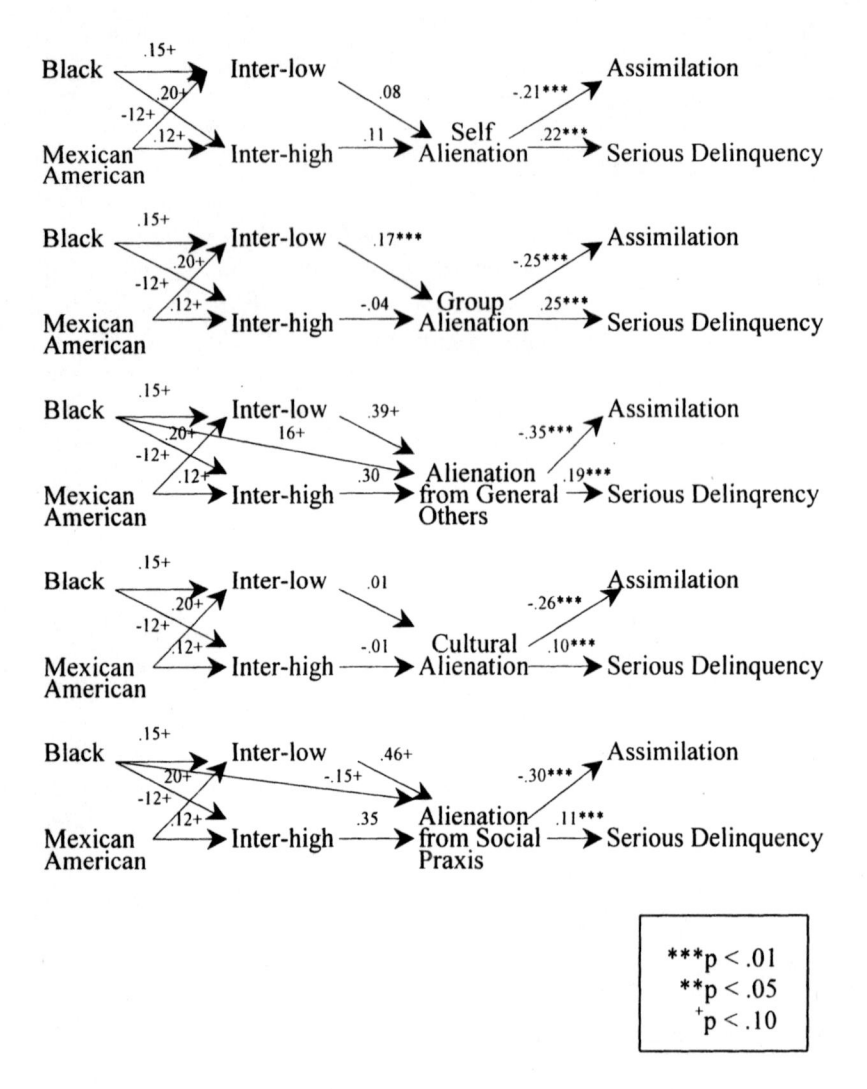

Figure 6.2 Causal model using the five measures of alienation and interaction terms based on perceived economic oppression and family support

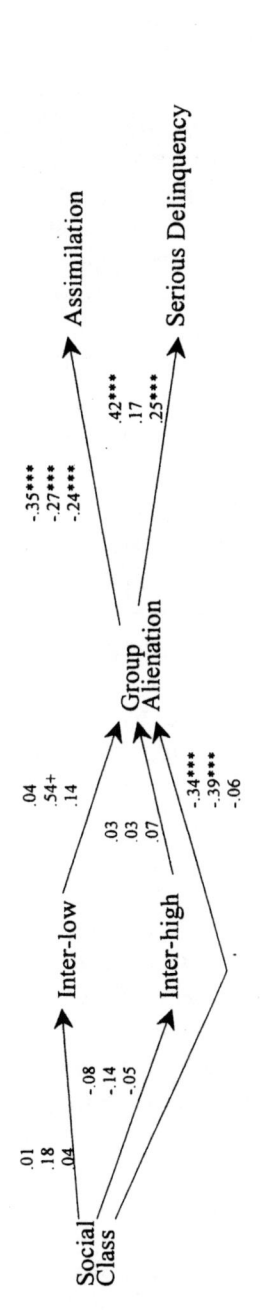

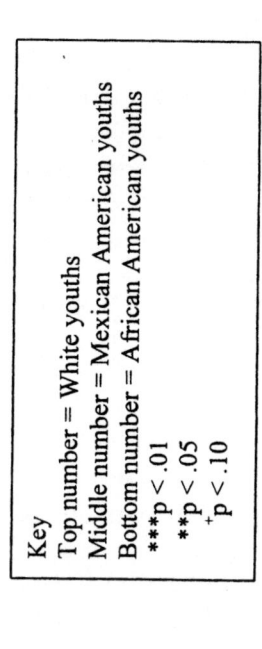

Figure 6.3 Causal model using alienation from racial or social group and serious delinquency

for all youths with few significant effects being found.

The models using alienation from the general other and alienation from the social praxis (see Figures 6.4 and 6.5), are more effective in explaining the delinquency of African American youths than Mexican American or White youths. Other than the insignificant effects of class on the interaction terms and the positive rather than inverse effects on inter-high on the alienation measures, all other results are as expected. More importantly, for African American youths the data show the hypothesized inverse effect of alienation on assimilation and positive effect of alienation on serious delinquency. For Mexican American and White youths, the alienation measures in these models do not significantly affect serious delinquency.

We also need to determine if the models are consistent with hypotheses when other types of delinquency are included in the analysis. In other words, do the alienation measures affect all or only some of the delinquency measures? To answer this question, we again re-estimate the models for each racial group using all five of the delinquency variables (see Figures 6.6, 6.7, and 6.8). In these analyses, we specifically focus on the paths from alienation to the delinquency measures since the other paths are the same as those of previous models and the measures of the other concepts do not change.

For African American youths, we find that alienation from the racial or social group and alienation from the general other are positively associated with the other four measures of delinquency. Alienation from the social praxis, however, only affects the serious and moderate delinquency of African American youths. For White youths, alienation from the racial or social group also has significant positive effects on moderate and minor delinquency, property crimes and alcohol use. When the causal model is estimated using the other measures of alienation, the path between alienation and delinquency remains insignificant regardless of the measure of delinquency being used. Finally, the analyses show that the path between alienation and delinquency is insignificant regardless of the measure of alienation or delinquency for Mexican American youths.

Summary

In this chapter, we tested a causal model of delinquency drawn from the neocolonial perspective. This model enabled us to examine the effects of

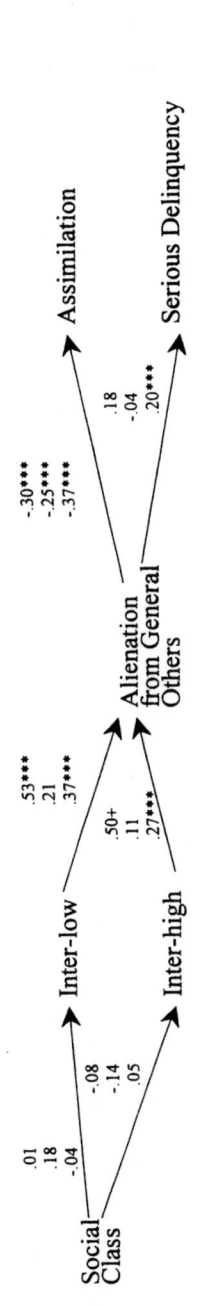

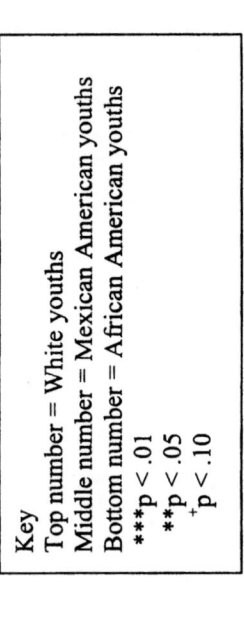

Figure 6.4 Causal model using alienation from the general other and serious delinquency

86   *Crime, Violence and Minority Youths*

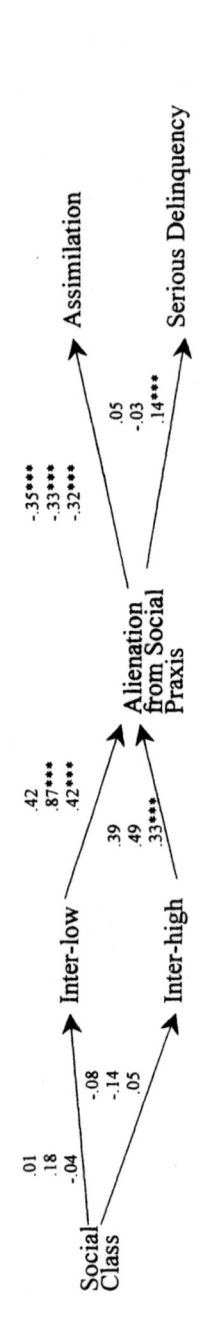

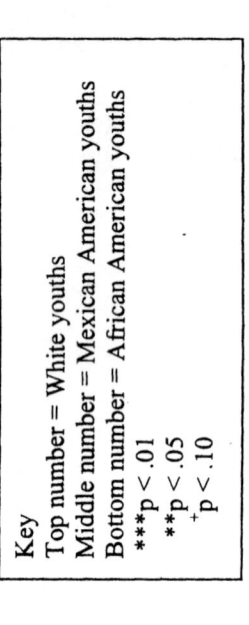

Figure 6.5   Causal model using alienation from social praxis and serious delinquency

race and class as separate constructs on the interrelationships among perceptual, attitudinal, and behavioral variables. Several hypothesized and implied relationships suggested by the causal model were not supported by the data. The race effects only approached statistical significance. In two cases, the direction of these findings contradicted theoretical expectations. Trends in the data reveal greater perceptions of economic oppression, higher levels of alienation from the general other, and lower levels of self-determination for White youths. These patterns point to the possibility of other variables variables influencing the association between race, perceived economic oppression and alienation. For example, affirmative action and diversity programs which attempt to increase structural opportunities for minorities may be viewed by White youths, especially those with low family support, as reverse discrimination or placing them at an 'unfair disadvantage'. This, in turn, could result in higher perceptions of alienation. Another possibility is that the effects of race on perceived oppression for youths with low levels of family support are actually the opposite of what is posited by the neocolonial model. That is, White youths, because of their higher racial status, have greater expectations of structural success than similarly situated African- and Mexican American youths, and thus have higher (rather than lower) perceptions of economic oppression.

Class was not a relevant variable in the causal model for the combined sample and only played a role in explaining alienation from the racial or social group for Mexican American and White youths. Thus, it appears that class is an important variable for making within group rather than across group comparisons. However, we see that the relationship between social class and alienation differs for African Americans in that no significant class variations in alienation are found for these individuals.

Third, cultural and self-alienation were not significantly associated with the interaction terms. The nonsignificance of cultural alienation may be attributed to the present shift in multiculturalism in American society. In the past decades, we have seen an emphasis on the inclusion of different cultural views and perspectives. Minority youths are being taught the importance of culture and to view their cultural heritage positively. While cultural alienation may have been a major source of alienation in past years, the events of recent years may have lessen its importance.

Finally, two factors may explain the insignificant association between self-alienation and the interaction terms. It is possible that youths

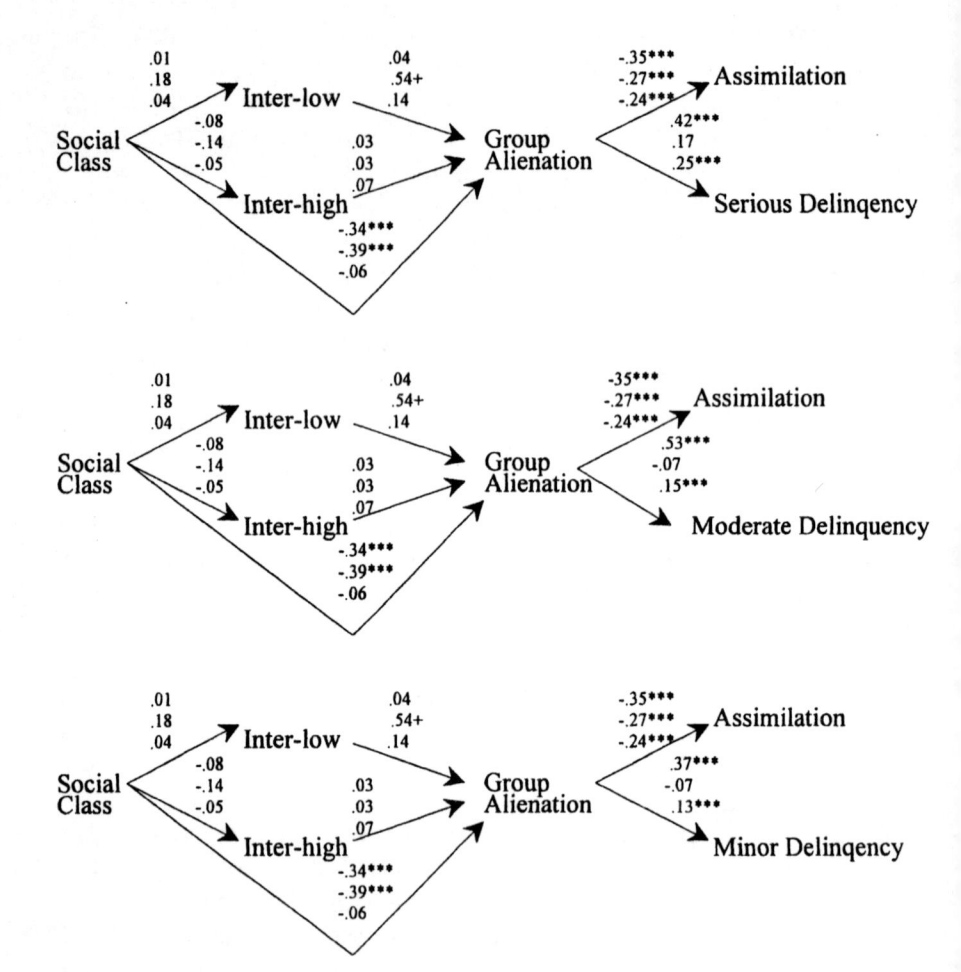

88 *Crime, Violence and Minority Youths*

Diagram 1 (Serious Delinquency)

Social Class → Inter-low: .01, .18, .04
Social Class → Inter-high: -.08, -.14, -.05
Inter-low → Group Alienation: .04, .54+, .14
Inter-high → Group Alienation: .03, .03, .07
Social Class → Group Alienation: -.34***, -.39***, -.06
Group Alienation → Assimilation: -.35***, -.27***, -.24***
Group Alienation → Serious Delinqency: .42***, .17, .25***

Diagram 2 (Moderate Delinquency)

Social Class → Inter-low: .01, .18, .04
Social Class → Inter-high: -.08, -.14, -.05
Inter-low → Group Alienation: .04, .54+, .14
Inter-high → Group Alienation: .03, .03, .07
Social Class → Group Alienation: -.34***, -.39***, -.06
Group Alienation → Assimilation: -.35***, -.27***, -.24***
Group Alienation → Moderate Delinquency: .53***, -.07, .15***

Diagram 3 (Minor Delinquency)

Social Class → Inter-low: .01, .18, .04
Social Class → Inter-high: -.08, -.14, -.05
Inter-low → Group Alienation: .04, .54+, .14
Inter-high → Group Alienation: .03, .03, .07
Social Class → Group Alienation: -.34***, -.39***, -.06
Group Alienation → Assimilation: -.35***, -.27***, -.24***
Group Alienation → Minor Delinqency: .37***, -.07, .13***

Pathways to Assimilation and Crime 89

(continued)

```
                    .01            .04              -.35***
                    .18            .54+             -.27***    Assimilation
                    .04   Inter-low .14             -.24***
                        -.08                      .39***
Social              -.14        .03    Group       -.06
Class               -.05        .03  Alienation    .17***
                        Inter-high .07                 Property Crimes
                              -.34***
                              -.39***
                              -.06
```

```
                    .01            .04              -.35***
                    .18            .54+             -.27***    Assimilation
                    .04   Inter-low .14             -.24***
                        -.08                      -.32***
Social              -.14        .03    Group       -.09
Class               -.05        .03  Alienation    .12***
                        Inter-high .07                 Alcohol Use
                              -.34***
                              -.39***
                              -.06
```

> Key: Top number = White youths
> Middle number = Mexican American youths
> Bottom number = African American youths
> ***p < .01
> **p < .05
> +p < .10

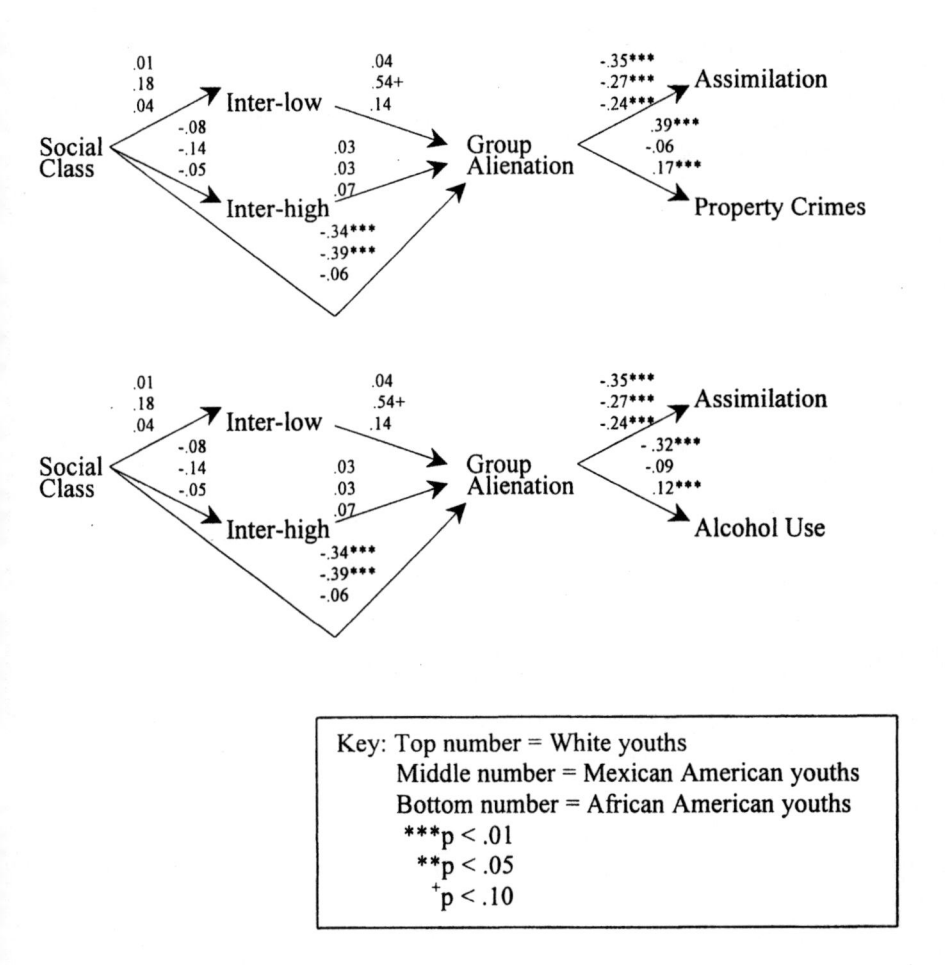

Figure 6.6 Causal model using alienation from racial or social group and all measures of delinquency for three racial groups

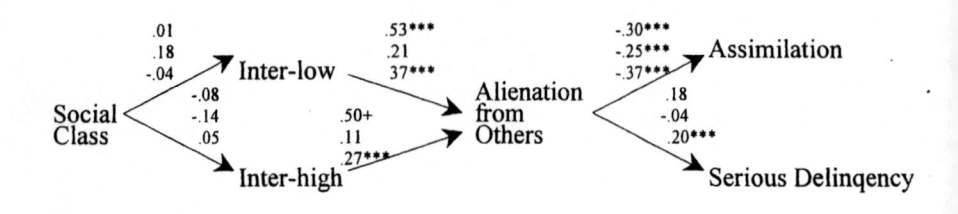

Figure 1

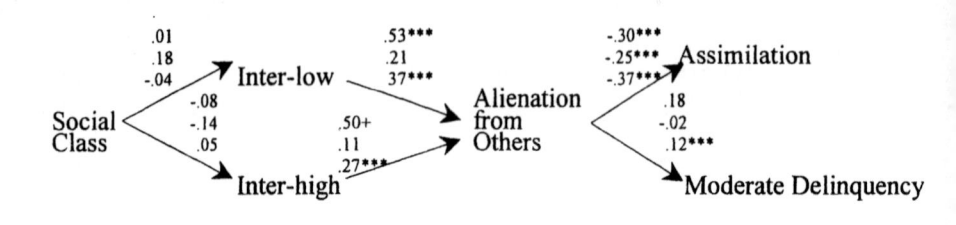

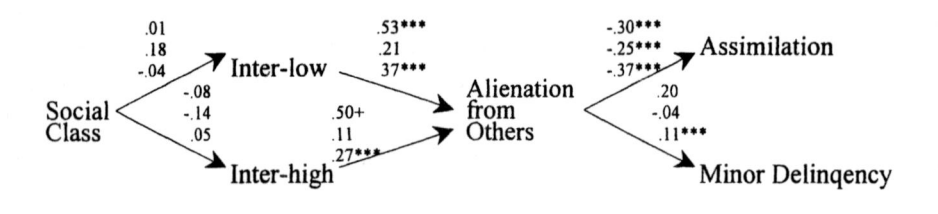

```
              .01        .53***           -.30***
              .18        .21              -.25***  Assimilation
              -.04 ↗Inter-low  ↘ .37***   -.37*** ↗
Social       -.08                  Alienation    .18
Class  ⟨     -.14       .50+       from          -.04
              .05       .11     ↗  Others        .20*** ↘
                 ↘Inter-high .27***                Serious Delinqency
```

```
              .01        .53***           -.30***
              .18        .21              -.25***  Assimilation
              -.04 ↗Inter-low  ↘ .37***   -.37*** ↗
Social       -.08                  Alienation    .18
Class  ⟨     -.14       .50+       from          -.02
              .05       .11     ↗  Others        .12*** ↘
                 ↘Inter-high .27***                Moderate Delinquency
```

```
              .01        .53***           -.30***
              .18        .21              -.25***  Assimilation
              -.04 ↗Inter-low  ↘ .37***   -.37*** ↗
Social       -.08                  Alienation    .20
Class  ⟨     -.14       .50+       from          -.04
              .05       .11     ↗  Others        .11*** ↘
                 ↘Inter-high .27***                Minor Delinqency
```

(continued)

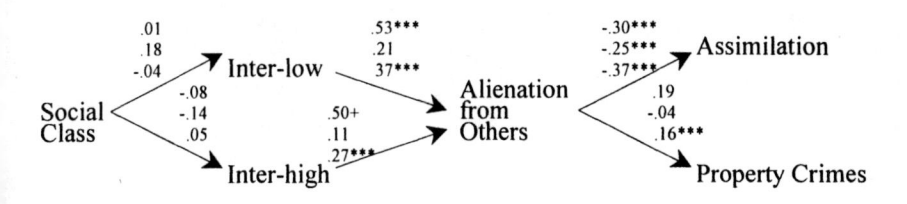

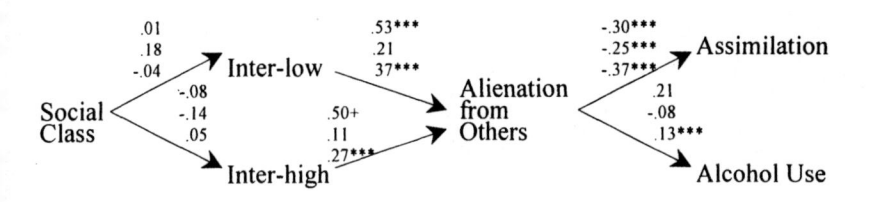

```
                    .01                 .53***          -.30***
                    .18                  .21            -.25***    Assimilation
                    -.04   Inter-low    .37***          -.37***
                         -.08                   Alienation   .19
Social             -.14          .50+           from         -.04
Class               .05          .11            Others       .16***
                         Inter-high  .27***                     Property Crimes
```

```
                    .01                 .53***          -.30***
                    .18                  .21            -.25***    Assimilation
                    -.04   Inter-low    .37***          -.37***
                         -.08                   Alienation   .21
Social             -.14          .50+           from         -.08
Class               .05          .11            Others       .13***
                         Inter-high  .27***                     Alcohol Use
```

> Key: Top number = White youths
> Middle number = Mexican American youths
> Bottom number = African American youths
> ***p < .01
> **p < .05
> +p < .10

Figure 6.7 Causal model using alienation from general other and all measures of delinquency for three racial groups

Crime, Violence and Minority Youths

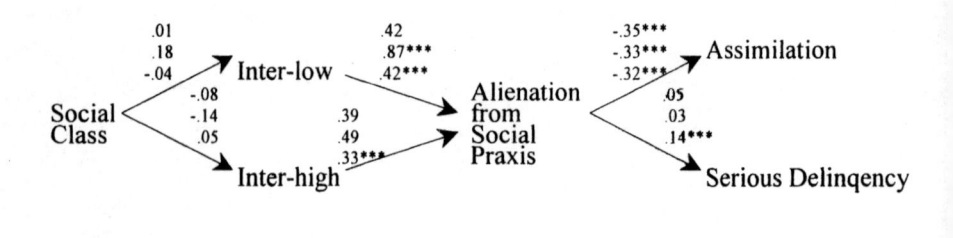

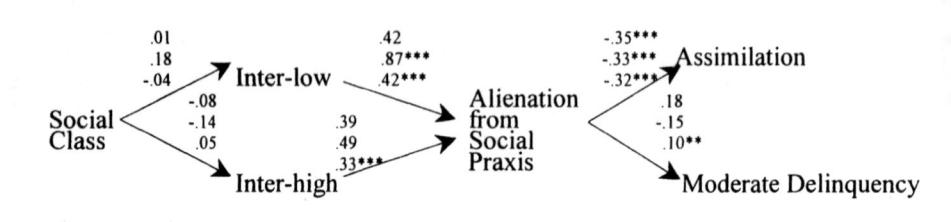

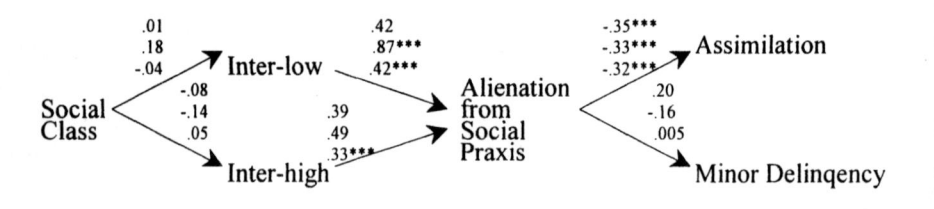

(continued)

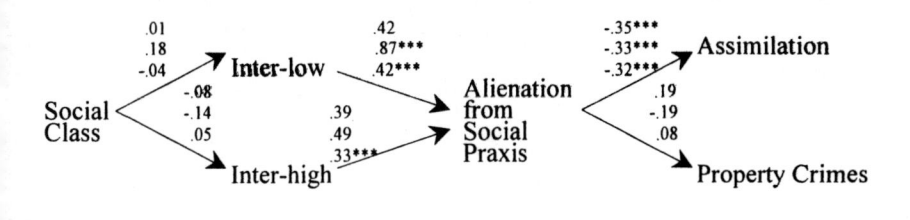

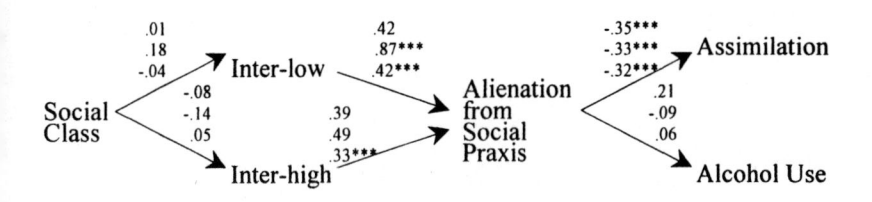

Figure 6.8 Causal model using alienation from social praxis and all measures of delinquency for three racial groups

Key: Top number = White youths
   Middle number = Mexican American youths
   Bottom number = African American youths
   ***$p < .01$
   **$p < .05$
   +$p < .10$

are less likely to report self-alienation than other types of alienation. This is reflective of discrimination research which shows that individuals are more likely to report group discrimination than individual discrimination (Sigelman and Welch, 1994). Thus, youths may find it more demeaning to report negative attitudes toward themselves. It is also plausible that self-alienation is not a factor for these youths.

7 Theoretical Promise of the Colonial Perspective

Introduction

In this study, we critically examined the ability of classic structural perspectives and the colonial model to explain traditional high rates of crime among minority youths. We argued that the classic models are deficient explanations of minority crime because they: a) confound the effects of race and class on behavior; b) are ahistorical; c) fail to account for differential responses to shared conditions; and d) measure strain as a global concept. Although the colonial model has been offered as an alternative explanation for Black crime and violence, theoretical shortcomings, some of which are common to the classic perspectives, also restrict its explanatory power. We propose the neocolonial model as a theoretical framework that addresses the limitations of both theoretical perspectives. The neocolonial model is empirically applied to a voluntary sample of African American, Mexican American and White youths. Below, we provide an overview of the major findings of these analyses and discuss the theoretical promise of a colonial perspective in criminology.

Examining the Results

Chapters 4-6 highlight the complexity of testing the neocolonial model. Arguably the greatest obstacle facing researchers is obtaining a sample with sufficient race and class variability. Our sample was racially skewed with much smaller distributions of White and Mexican American youths. Moreover, our sample only contained nine lower-class White youths. These weaknesses reduce our ability to make comparisons across race, class, and race and class groups, and attenuate any conclusions that are drawn from the findings. The extensiveness of the propositions and assumptions of the perspective further restricted our analyses.

One of the major premises of the neocolonial model is the independent and interactive effects of race and class on perceived oppression, alienation and social support. According to the perspective, the intensity of these variables will vary among youths according to their position (e.g., race, class, and race and class) in the structural hierarchy. As we saw in Chapter 5, the data provided limited support for these expectations. No significant social class effects were found.

Significant race and interaction effects were few, appeared to associated with particular measures, and were often contradictory. For example, variations in perceived social oppression were only associated with race. In line with expectations, African American youths reported higher levels of perceived social support than Mexican American and White youths. However, the failure to find variations in perceived social oppression among Mexican American and White youths suggests that perceived oppression does not always vary across majority and minority group members. Moreover, the variation in the intensity of the variables among the three racial groups (low, intermediate and high), as posited by the neocolonial model, was not reflected by the data.

Other variations among youths also contradicted theoretical expectations. Of the three racial groups, White youths reported the highest levels of alienation from the general other. Lower-class African American youths expressed lower levels of self-alienation than their Mexican American counterparts. In Chapter 6, we saw that White youths with low levels of family support were more likely to view themselves as being the victims of economic oppression than African- or Mexican American youths. Also, White youths expressed higher levels of alienation from the general other and lower self-determination than African American youths. These contradictory findings suggest that other variables apart from the independent and interactive effects of race and class influence these associations and point to the importance of describing the social contexts in which these findings occur. The findings further elude to the primacy of class in analysis across different race and class categories.

Findings reported in Chapter 6 further highlighted the applicability of variables in the perspective in particular contexts. For example, social class was an insignificant factor for the combined sample but accounted for differences in alienation from the racial or social group for Mexican

American and White youths when the causal model was analyzed by race. Analysis for the combined sample also showed that the interaction terms did not significantly affect self- or cultural alienation, implying that certain variants of the variable are more applicable than others in the delinquency process.

Finally, the findings questioned the role of social support in the association between perceived oppression and alienation. As shown in Chapter 6, both interaction terms positively affected alienation from the general other and alienation from the social praxis. The data appear to suggest that family support has an additive rather buffering effect; that is, all levels of family support attenuate the effect of perceived oppression on alienation to some extent.

The race effects on the second interaction term (inter-high) as well as the effects of the alienation measures on assimilation and serious delinquency, provide some of the strongest support for the neocolonial model. In line with hypotheses, African- and Mexican American youths with high levels of family support expressed greater perceptions of economic oppression than White youths. Most importantly, the data for the combined sample repeatedly revealed an inverse association between the alienation measures and assimilation and a positive association between alienation and serious delinquency.

As an explanation of minority crime, the neocolonial model appears to be more effective in explaining the delinquency of African American youths. This holds true even when different types of delinquency are analyzed. Although the variables in the causal model are applicable to Mexican Americans, to explain Mexican American delinquency, other characteristics of their colonization or collective experiences undoubtedly need to be incorporated into the analysis.

Theoretical Promise of the Colonial Perspective

The neocolonial model theorizes the role of race and class in adolescent crime and violence. Racial status is addressed from a historical standpoint while differential responses to shared oppressive conditions are explained by varying levels in social support. Although initial tests yield limited empirical support for the perspective, the findings of the pilot study provide some general implications for the study of crime and delinquency. First, the study shows the importance of analyzing the independent effects of race and class. Findings from the ANOVA analysis shows that these variables affect different factors. Findings from the causal model also suggest that race and class play different roles when making within and across group comparisons.

Second, the study illustrates the salience of variables such as perceived oppression and alienation in explaining delinquency in general, and African American delinquency in particular. Although this arguably has also been done by classic structural perspectives, the pilot test stressed the importance of focusing on specific dimensions of perceived oppression and alienation and their role in certain types of delinquency.

Third, the pilot study implies that researchers should focus on race specific rather than general explanations of delinquency even for racial minorities. Although the findings provide limited support for significant differences among the youths in regards to perceived oppression, social support systems and alienation, they do show that these variables behave differently in explaining the delinquency of the three racial groups. This also points to the fact that the neocolonial model, as presented, does not provide an universal explanation of delinquency for all minority groups.

And finally, the study makes some specific implications regarding the adequacy of the neocolonial model. The results suggested that the perspective must give further consideration to the effects of race and class on the variables in the neocolonial model across and within racial categories. Arguments regarding racial variations among youths with an absence or low levels of family support and racial variations for particular measures of alienation appear to be too simplistic. Researchers need to carefully explore other factors that may influence these associations. Last, the data suggested a reduction in the measures of alienation from five to three at least for adolescent populations.

Because of data limitations, these findings and implications should be viewed cautiously. Our analyses primarily serves as a temporal benchmark for future research examining the link between colonialism and crime. The complexity of the theoretical model will require the collection of other data to fully test its propositions and assumptions. We recommend, however, that much smaller analyses be undertaken with primary efforts being focused on obtaining an adequate sample. Also, several other issues have been raised for future research. These issues include 1) the application of the perspective to other racial minorities, 2) the application of the perspective to females, and 3) the examination of the role of other types of social support (e.g., the African American church) in crime and violence.

References

Acosta-Belen, E. and B. Sjostrom (1988) *The Hispanic Experience in the United States: Contemporary Issues and Perspectives*. New York: Praeger.

Acuna, R. (1972) *Occupied America: The Chicano Struggle Toward Liberation*. San Francisco, CA: Canfield.

Agnew, R. (1992) 'Foundation for a General Strain Theory of Crime and Delinquency', *Criminology*, vol. 30, pp. 47-86.

Aguirre, A. and J. Turner (1995) *American Ethnicity: The Dynamics and Consequences of Racism*. New York: McGraw-Hill.

Alvarez, R. (1973) 'The Psycho-historical and Socioeconomic Development of the Chicano Community in the United States', *Social Science Quarterly*, vol. 53, pp. 920-942.

Anderson, E. (1990) *Streetwise: Race, Class and Change in an Urban Community*. Chicago, IL: University of Chicago Press.

Anderson, L. (1991) 'Acculturative Stress: A Theory of Relevance to Black Americans', *Clinical Psychology Review*, vol. 11, pp. 685-695.

Austin, R. (1983) 'The Colonial Model, Subcultural Theory, and Intragroup Violence', *Journal of Criminal Justice*, vol. 11, pp. 93-104.

----- (1987) 'Progress Toward Racial Inequality and Reduction of Black Criminal Violence', *Journal of Criminal Justice*, vol. 11, pp. 437-459.

Babbie, E. (1992) *The Practice of Social Research*. Belmont, CA: Wadsworth Publishing Company.

Barrera, M. (1979) *Race and Class in the Southwest*. Notre Dame, IND: University of Notre Dame Press.

Bean, F. and M. Tienda (1987) *The Hispanic Population in the United States*. New York: Russell Sage Foundation.

Berger, R. (1995) *The Sociology of Juvenile Delinquency*. 2nd edition. Chicago, IL: Nelson-Hall.

References

Billingsley, A. (1968) *Black Families in White America*. Englewood Cliffs, NJ: Prentice-Hall.

Blackwell, J. (1985) *The Black Community: Diversity and Unity*. 2nd edition. New York: Harper and Collins Publishers.

----- (1991) *The Black Community: Diversity and Unity*. 3rd edition. New York: Harper and Collins Publishers.

----- and P. Hart (1982) *Cities, Suburbs and Blacks: A Study of Concerns, Distrust and Alienation*. New York: General Hall, Inc.

Blauner, R. (1972) *Racial Oppression in America*. New York: Harper and Row.

----- (1992) 'The Ambiguities of Racial Change', in M. Anderson and P. Collins (eds.) *Race, Class and Gender*. Belmont, CA: Wadsworth Publishing Company, pp. 54-65.

----- (1994) 'Colonized and Immigrant Minorities', in R. Takaki (ed.) *From Different Shores: Perspectives on Race and Ethnicity in America*. New York: Oxford University Press, pp. 149-160.

Blea, I. (1988) *Toward a Chicano Social Science*. New York: Praeger.

Bluestone, G. (1988) 'Deindustrialization and Unemployment in America', *The Review of the Black Political Economy*, vol. 17(2), pp. 29-44.

Boamah-Wiafe, D. (1990) *The Black Experience in Contemporary America*. Omaha, NE: Wisdoms.

Boykin, A. and C. Ellison (1994) 'The Multiple Ecologies of Black Youth Socialization: An Afrographic Analysis', in R. Taylor (ed.) *African American Youths: Their Social and Economic Status in the United States*. New York: Praeger, pp. 93-128.

Bulhan, H. (1985) *Frantz Fanon and the Psychology of Oppression*. New York: Plenum.

Bureau of the Census (1993) *Current Population Reports: U. S. Population Estimates By Age, Sex, Race and Hispanic Origin*. Washington, D. C.: U. S. Department of Commerce.

Bureau of Justice Statistics (1994) *Criminal Victimization in the United States, 1993*. Washington, D.C.: U. S. Department of Justice.

Calabrese, R. (1989) 'The Effects of Mobility on Adolescent Alienation', *The High School Journal*, Oct/Nov, pp. 41-45.

Carmichael, S. and C. Hamiliton (1967) *Black Power: The Politics of Liberation in America*. New York: Random House.

Carr, R.(1984) *Puerto Rico: A Colonial Experiment*. New York: New York University Press.
Carson, C. (1995) *In Struggle: SNCC and the Black Awakening of the 1960s*. Cambridge, MASS: Harvard University Press.
Clark, K. (1965) *Dark Ghetto: The Dilemmas of Social Power*. 2nd edition. Hanover, NH: Wesleyan University Press.
Cloward, R. and L. Ohlin (1960) *Delinquency and Opportunity: A Theory of Delinquent* Gangs. New York: The Free Press.
Cochran, M. (1990) 'Environmental Factors Constraining Network Development', in M. Cochran, M. Larner, D. Riley, L. Gunnarsson and C. Henderson, Jr. (eds.) *Extending Families: The Social Network of Parents and Children*. Cambridge, MASS: Cambridge University Press, pp. 277-296.
Cohen, A. (1955) *Delinquent Boys: The Culture of the Gang*. New York: The Free Press.
Cross, W. (1990) 'Race and Ethnicity: Effects on Social Networks', in M. Cochran, M. Larner, D. Riley and C. Henderson, Jr. (eds.) *Extending Families: The Social Networks of Parents and Children*. Cambridge, MASS: Cambridge University Press, pp. 67-85.
Cullen, F. (1994) 'Social Support as an Organizing Concepts for Criminology: Presidential Address to the Academy of Criminal Justice Sciences', *Justice Quarterly*, vol. 11(4), pp. 527-559.
Curry, E. (1976) *Significant Other Influence and Career Decisions: Black and White Male Youths, Volume 1*. Columbus, OH: National Center for Research in Vocational Education.
Dawson, M. (1994) *Behind the Mule: Race and Class in African American Politics*. Princeton, NJ: Princeton University Press.
Dean, D. (1961) 'Alienation: Its Meaning and Measurement', *American Sociological Review*, vol. 26, pp. 753-758.
Dubois, W. E. B. (1962) *Black Reconstruction in America: 1860-1880*. New York: Maxwell MacMillan International.
Einstadter, W. and S. Henry (1994) *Criminological Theory: An Analysis of Underlying Assumptions*. Forth Worth, TX: Harcourt Brace College Publishers.
Elliott, D. and S. Ageton (1980) 'Reconciling Race and Class Differences in Self-Reported and Official Estimates of Delinquency', *American Sociological Review*, vol. 45, pp. 95-110.

Fanon, F. (1963) *The Wretched of the Earth*. New York: Grove Press.
----- (1967) *Black Skin, White Masks*. New York: Grove Press.
Farnworth, M., T. Thornberry, M. Krohn and A. Lizotte (1994) 'Measurement in the Study of Class and Delinquency: Integrating Theory and Research', *Journal of Research in Crime and Delinquency*, vol. 31(1): pp. 32-51.
Feagin, J. (1978) *Racial and Ethnic Relations*. New York: Prentice-Hall.
----- and C. Feagin (1996) *Racial and Ethnic Relations*. 5th edition. Upper Saddle River, NJ: Prentice-Hall.
----- and H. Vera (1995) *White Racism: The Basics*. New York: Routledge Press.
Federal Bureau of Investigation (1991) *Crime in the United States, 1990*. Washington, D.C.: Government Printing Office.
Frazier, E. (1957) *Race and Culture Contacts in the Modern World*. Boston, MASS: Beacon Press.
----- (1974) *The Negro Church in America*. New York: Schocken.
Gary, L., D. Brown, N. Milburn, F. Ahmed and J. Booth (1989) *Depression in Black American Adults: Findings from the Norfolk Area Health Study (Final Report)*. Washington, D. C.: Institute for Urban Affairs and Research.
Genelin, M. and B. Coplen (1989) *Los Angeles Street Grangs: Report Recommendations of the County-Wide Criminal Justice Coordination Committee Interagency Gang Task Force, March 1989*. Los Angeles, CA: Interagency Task Force.
Gentry, W. and S. Kobasa (1984) 'Social and Psychological Resources Mediating Stress-Illness Relationships in Humans', in W. Gentry (ed.) *Handbook of Behavioral Medicine*. New York: Guilford Press, pp. 97-113.
Gibbs, J. (1990) 'Developing Intervention Models for Black Families: Linking Theory and Research', in H. Cheatham and J. Steward (eds.) *Black Families: Interdisciplinary Perspectives*. New Brunswick, NJ: Transaction Press, pp. 153-173.
Glasgow, D. (1981) *The Black Underclass: Poverty, Unemployment, and Entrapment of Ghetto Youth*. New Brunswick, NJ: Transaction Press.
Hacker, A. (1992) *Two Nations: Black and White, Separate, Hostile and Unequal*. New York: Charles Scribner's Sons.

Hagan, J., A. Gillis and J. Simpson (1985) 'The Class Structure of Gender and Delinquency: Toward a Power-Control Theory of Common Delinquency', *American Journal of Sociology*, vol. 90, pp. 1115-1178.

Hawkins, D. and N. Jones (1988) 'Black Adolescents and the Criminal Justice System', in R. Jones (ed.), *Black Adolescents*. Berkeley, CA: Cobb and Henry, pp. 325-340.

Hendin, H. (1987) 'Youth Suicide: A Psychological Perspective', *Suicide in Life Threatening Behavior*, vol. 17, pp. 151-156.

Hirschi, T. (1969) *Causes of Delinquency*. Berkeley, CA: University of California Press.

Hochschild, J. (1995) *Race, Class and the Soul of the Nation*. Princeton, NJ: Princeton University Press.

Holahan, C., D. Valentiner, and R. Moss (1995) 'Parental Support, Coping Strategies and Psychololgical Adjustment: An Integrative Model with Late Adolescents', *Journal of Youth and Adolescents*, vol. 24(6): pp. 633-648.

Hoppe, J. and D. Heller (1975) 'Alienation, Familism and the Utilization of Health Services By Mexican Americans', *Journal of Health and Social Behavior*, vol. 16, pp. 304-314.

Huizinga, D. and D. Elliott (1987) 'Juvenile Offenders: Prevalence, Offender Incidence, and Arrest Rates by Race', *Crime and Delinquency*, 33, pp. 206-223.

Jaynes, G. and R. Williams (1989) *A Common Destiny: Blacks in American Society*. Washington, D.C.: National Academy Press.

Kirschenman, J. and K. Neckerman (1991) 'We'd Love to Hire Them But...: The Meaning of Race for Employers', in C. Jencks and P. E. Peterson (eds.), *The Urban Underclass*. Washington, D.C.: Brookings Institute, pp. 203-32.

Long, S. (1976) 'Political Alienation Among Black and White Adolescents: A Test of the Social Deprivation and Political Reality Models', *American Politics Quarterly*, vol. 4(3), pp. 267-303.

Marger, M. (1994) *Race and Ethnic Relations: American and Global Perspectives*. Belmont, CA: Wadsworth Publishing Company.

Martinez, R. (1996) 'Latinos and Lethal Violence: The Impact of Poverty and Inequality', *Social Problems*, vol. 43(2), pp. 131-145.

Massey, D. and N. Denton (1987) 'Trends in the Residential Segregation of Blacks, Hispanics and Asians', *American Sociological Review*, vol. 52, pp. 802-825.

----- and ----- (1993) *American Apartheid: Segregation and the Making of the Underclass*. Cambridge, MASS: Harvard University Press.

----- and B. Mullan (1984) 'Processes of Hispanic and Black Spatial Assimilation', *American Journal of Sociology*, vol. 89(4), pp. 836-873.

McIntosh, P. (1992) 'White Privilege and Male Privilege: A Personal Account of Comming to See Correspondence Through Work in Women Studies', in M. Anderson and P. Collins (eds.) *Race, Class and Gender*. Belmont, CA: Wadsworth Publishing, pp. 70-81.

Merton, R. (1938) 'Social Structure and Anomie', *American Sociological Review*, vol. 26, pp. 753-758.

Milburn, N. (1982) 'Individual, Organizational and Individual-Organization Fit Characteristics and Their Relationship to Participation in Neighborhood Associations'. Ph.D. Dissertation, University of Michigan at Ann Arbor.

Miller, D. (1991) *Handbook of Research Design and Social Measurement*. 5th edition. Thousand Oaks, CA: Sage Publications.

Mincy, R. (1994) *Nuturing Young Black Males*. Washington, D.C.: The Urban Institute Press.

Miron, L. and M. Lauria (1995) 'Identity Politics and Student Resistance to Inner City Public Schooling', *Youth and Society*, vol. 27(1), pp. 29-54.

Moore, J. (1970) 'Colonialism: The Case of Mexican Americans', *Social Problems*, vol. 17, pp. 463-472.

----- and R. Pinderhughes (1993) *In the Barrios: Latinos and the Underclass Debate*. New York: Russell Sage Foundation.

----- and D. Vigil (1993) 'Barrios in Transition', in J. Moore and R. Pinderhughes (eds.) *In the Barriors: Latinos and the Underclass Debate*. New York: Russell Sage Foundation, pp. 27-49.

Moyer, T. and R. Motta (1982) 'Alienation and School Adjustment Among Black and White Adolescents', *The Journal of Psychology*, vol. 112, pp. 21-28.

Murguia, E. (1975) *Assimilation, Colonialism and the Mexican People*. Austin, TX: The University of Texas Press.

Myers, H. (1989) 'Urban Stress and Mental Health in Black Youth: An Epidemiological and Conceptual Update', in R. Jones (ed.) *Black Adolescent*. Berkeley, CA: Cobb and Henry, pp. 123-152.

National Research Council (1993) *Losing Generations: Adolescents in High-Risks Settings*. Washington, D.C.: National Academy Press.

Obu, J. (1991) 'Minority Coping Responses and School Experience', *Journal of Psychohistory*, vol. 18(4), pp. 433-456.

Oliver, Melvin and T. Shapiro (1995) *Black Wealth/White Wealth: A New Perspective on Racial Inequality*. New York: Routledge.

Padilla, F. (1993) 'The Quest for Community: Puerto Ricans in Chicago', in J. Moore and R. Pinderhughes (eds.) *In the Barrios: Latinos and the Underclass Debate*. New York: Russell Sage Foundation.

Park, R. and E. Burgess (1925) *The City*. Chicago, IL: University of Chicago Press.

Pettigrew, T. (1980) 'The Changing--not declining--Significance of Race', *Contemporary Sociology*, vol. 9, pp. 19-21.

Quinn, J. (1994) 'Traditional Youth Service Systems and Their Work With Young Black Males', in R. Mincy (ed.) *Nuturing Young Black Males*. Washington, D.C.: The Urban Institute Press, pp. 119-150.

Reed, W. (1993) *African Americans: Essential Perspectives*. Westport, CT: Auburn House.

Rodriquez, N. (1993) 'Economic Restructuring and Latino Growth in Houston', in J. Moore and R. Pinderhughes (eds.) *In the Barrios: Latinos and the Underclass Debate*. New York: Russell Sage Foundation, pp. 101-128.

Rodriguez, O. and D. Weisburn (1991) 'The Integrated Social Control Model and Ethnicity: The Case of Puerto Rican American Delinquency', *Criminal Justice and Behavior*, vol. 18(4), pp. 464-479.

Rook, K. and D. Dooley (1982) 'Applying Social Support Research: Theoretical Problems and Future Directions', *Journal of Social Issues*, vol. 3(1), pp. 5-28.

Rose, P. (1990) *They and We: Racial and Ethnic Relations in the United States*. New York: McGraw-Hill.

Rubin, R., A. Billingsley and C. Caldwell (1991) 'The Role of the Black Church in Working with Black Adolescents', *Adolescence*, vol. 29(1), pp. 251-266.

Russell, K. (1992) 'Development of A Black Criminology and the Role of the Black Criminologists', *Justice Quarterly*, vol. 9(4), pp. 667-683.
Sampson, R. and B. Groves (189) 'Community Structure and Crime: Testing Social-Disorganization Theory', *American Journal of Sociology*, vol. 4, pp. 774-802.
Seeman, M. (1959) 'On the Meaning of Alienation', *American Sociological Review*, vol. 24, pp. 783-791.
Shaw, C. and H. McKay (1942) *Juvenile Delinquency and Urban Areas*. Chicago, IL: University of Chicago Press.
----- and ----- (1969) *Juvenile Delinquency and Urban Areas*. Revised edition. Chicago, IL: University of Chicago Press.
Sigleman, L. and S. Welch (1994) *Black Americans' Views of Racial Inequality: The Dream Deferred*. New York: Cambridge University Press.
Skerry, P. (1993) *Mexican Americans: The Ambivalent Minority*. Cambridge, MASS: Harvard University Press.
Smart, J. and D. Smart (1995) 'Acculturative Stress of Hispanics: Loss and Challenge', *Journal of Counseling Development*, vol. 73, pp. 309-396.
Smith, K. (1974) 'Forming Composite Scales and Estimating Their Validity Through Factor Analysis', *Social Forces*, vol. 53(2), pp. 168-179.
Snyder, H. and M. Sickmund (1993) *Juvenile Offenders and Victims: A National Report*. Washington, D.C.: Office of Juvenile Justice and Delinquency Prevention.
Sommers, I., J. Fagan and D. Baskin (1994) 'The Influence of Acculturation and Familism on Puerto Rican Delinquency', *Justice Quarterly*, vol. 11(2), pp. 207-228.
Southwell, P. (1985) 'Alienation and Nonvoting in the United States: A Refined Operationalization', *Western Political Quarterly*, vol. 38(4), pp. 663-677.
Spaights, E. and G. Simpson (1986) 'Some Unique Causes of Black Suicide', *Psychology: A Quarterly Journal of Human Behavior*, vol. 23, pp. 1-5.

Spencer, M. (1995) 'Old Issues and New Theorizing About African American Youths: A Phenomenological Variant of Ecological System Theory', in R. Taylor (ed.) *African American Youth: Their Social and Economic Status in the United States.* Westport, CONN: Praeger, pp. 35-38.

Srole, L. (1956) 'Social Integration and Certain Corrollaries', *American Sociological Review*, vol. 21, pp. 709-716.

Stack, C. (1974) *All Our Kin.* New York: Harper and Row.

Staples, R. (1975) 'White Racism, Black Crime and American Justice: An Application of the Colonial Model to Explain Race and Crime', *Phylon*, vol. 36, pp. 14-22.

----- (1987) *The Urban Plantation: Racism and Colonialism in the Post Civil Rights Era.* Oakland, CA: The Black Scholar Press.

Steel, L. (1991) 'Early Work Experience Among White and Non-White Youths: Implications for Subsequent Enrollment and Employment', *Youth and Society*, vol. 22(4), pp. 419-447.

Sum, A., P. Harrington and W. Goedicke (1987) 'One-Fifth of the Nation's Teenagers: Employment Problems of Poor Youths in American', *Youth and Society*, vol. 18(3), pp. 195-237.

Tatum, B. (1994) 'The Colonial Model as a Theoretical Explanation of Crime and Delinquency', in A. Sulton (ed.) *African American Perspectives on Crime Causation, Criminal Justice Administration and Crime Prevention.* Englewood, CO: Sulton Lecture Series, pp. 33-52.

Taylor, R. (1995) *African American Youths: Their Social and Economic Status in the United States.* New York: Praeger.

Taylor, R. and L. Chatters (1991) 'Non-organizational Religious Participation Among Elderly Blacks', *Journal of Gerontology: Social Science*, vol. 31, pp. 15-30.

Telles, E. and E. Murguia (1990) 'Phenotypic Discrimination and Income Differences Among Mexican Americans', *Social Science Quarterly*, vol. 71, pp. 682-696.

Thornberry, T., A. Lizotte, M. Krohn and M. Farnworth (1980) *Student Interview Schedule: Rochester Youth Development Study.* Albany, NY: Hindelang Research Center.

Turner, J., R. Singleton and D. Musick (1990) *Oppression: A Socio-History of Black-White Relations in America.* Chicago, IL: Nelson-Hall.

Turner, M., M. Fix and R. Struyk (1991) *Opportunities Denied, Opportunities Diminished: Racial Discrimination in Hiring.* Washington, D.C.: The Urban Institute.

U. S. Department of Justice (1992) *Criminal Victimizations in the United States, 1991.* Washington, D. C.: Government Printing Office.

Valdez, A. (1993) 'Persistent Poverty, Crime, and Drugs: U.S.-Mexican Border Region', in J. Moore and R. Pinderhughes (eds.) *In the Barrios: Latinos and the Underclass Debate.* New York: Russell Sage Foundation, pp. 173-194.

Vander Zanden, J. (1972) *American Minority Relations.* New York: McGraw-Hill.

Velez-Ibanez, C. (1993) 'U. S. Mexicans in the Borderlands: Being Poor Without the Underclass', in J. Moore and R. Pinderhughes (eds.) *In the Barrios: Latinos and the Underclass Debate.* New York: Russell Sage Foundation, pp. 195-220.

Vernon, S. and R. Roberts (1985) 'A Comparison of Anglos and Mexican Americans on Selected Measures of Social Support', *Hispanic Journal of Behavioral Sciences*, vol. 7, pp. 381-399.

Vold, G., T. Bernard, and J. Snipes (1998) *Theoretical Criminology.* New York: Oxford University Press.

Williams, F. and M. McShane (1998) *Criminological Theory: Selected Readings.* 2nd edition. Cincinnati, OH: Anderson Publishing.

Wilson, W. (1973) *Power, Racism and Privilege: Race Relations in Theoretical and Sociohistorical Perspectives.* New York: The Free Press.

----- (1980) *The Declining Significance of Race: Blacks and Changing American Institutions.* Chicago, IL: University of Chicago Press.

----- (1987) *The Truly Disadvantaged: The Inner City, The Underclass, and Public Policy.* Chicago, IL: University of Chicago Press.

Bibliography

Alston, J. and M. Knapp (1974) 'Intergenerational Mobility Among Black Americans: Background Factors and Attitudinal Consequences', *Journal of Black Studies*, vol. 4(3), pp. 285-302.

Andersson, L. (1986) 'A Model of Estrangement: Including a Theoretical Understanding of Loneliness', *Psychological Reports*, vol. 58, pp. 683-695.

Block, C. (1988) 'Lethal Violence in the Chicago Community, 1965 to 1981', in Research Conference Proceedings, *Violence and Homicide in Hispanic Communities*, University of California Press, pp. 31-66.

Brooks, R. L. (1990) *Rethinking The American Race Problem*. Berkeley, CA: University of California Press.

Carmichael, S. and C. Hamilton (1967) *Black Power: The Politics of Liberation in America*. New York: Random House.

Chavez, E., R. Edwards and E. Oetting (1989) 'Mexican American and White American School Dropouts' Drug Use, Health Status, and Involvement in Violence', *Public Health Reports*, vol. 104, pp. 594-604.

Clayton, Obie (1996) *An American Dilemma Revisited: Race Relations in a Changing World*. New York: Russell Sage Foundation.

Comer, J. and A. Poussaint (1992) *Raising Black Children*. New York: Penguin Books.

Cross, W. E. (1991) *Shades of Black: Diversity in African American Identity*. Philadelphia, PA: Temple University Press.

Fanon, F. (1967) *A Dying Colonialism*. New York: Grove Press.

Feagin, J. and M. Sikes (1994) *Living With Racism: The Black Middle-Class Experience*. Boston, MASS: Beacon Press.

Franklin, J. (1976) *Racial Inequality in America*. Columbia, Missouri: University of Missouri Press.

Gordon, L., T. Sharpley-Whiting and R. White (1996) *Fanon: A Critical Reader*. Cambridge, MASS: Blackwell Publishers.

Hofstetter, C. and T. Buss (1988) 'Race and Alienation: Observations on the Impact of Joblessness', *Ethnic and Racial Studies*, vol. 11(3), pp. 305-318.

Jenkins, A. (1995) *Turning Corners: The Psychology of African Americans*. Boston, MASS: Allyn and Bacon.

Krause, N. and T. Tran (1989) 'Stress and Religious Involvement Among Older Blacks', *Journal of Gerontology: Social Sciences*, vol. 44, pp. 4-13.

Lyman, S. (1972) *The Black American in Sociological Thought*. New York: B. P. Putnam's Sons.

Middleton, R. (1963) 'Alienation, Race and Education', *American Sociological Review*, vol. 26, pp. 753-758.

Moore, J. (1989) 'Is There a Hispanic Underclass?', *Social Science Quarterly*, vol. 70, pp. 265-283.

----- and D. Vigil (1987) 'Chicano Gangs: Group Norms and Individual Factors Related to Adult Criminality', *Aztlan*, vol. 18, pp. 27-44.

National Council of La Raza (1992) *State of Hispanic America 1991: An Overview*. Washington, D.C.: National Council of La Raza.

Oliver, W. (1989) 'Sexual Conquest and Patterns of Black-on-Black Violence: A Structural-Cultural Perspective', *Violence and Victims*, vol. 4, pp. 257-271.

Page, C. (1996) *Showing My Color: Impolite Essays on Race and Identity*. New York: Harper and Collins Publishers.

Perkins, U. (1975) *Home is a Dirty Street: The Social Oppression of Black Children*. Chicago, IL: Third World Press.

Quarles, B. (1987) *The Negro in the Making of America*. New York: Simon and Schuster.

Rodgers, H. (1974) 'Toward an Explanation of the Political Efficacy and Political Cynicism of Black Adolescents: An Exploratory Study, *American Journal of Political Science*, vol. 11, pp. 257-282.

Ross, C. and J. Mirowsky (1987) 'Normlessness, Powerlessness, and Trouble with the Law', *Criminology*, vol. 25(4), pp. 257-269.

Sampson, R. (1987) 'Urban Black Violence: The Effect of Male Joblessness and Family Disruption', *American Journal of Sociology*, vol. 93(2), pp. 348-382.

Schaff, A. (1980) *Alienation as a Social Phenomenon*. Oxford, MASS: Pergamon Press.

Sheu, J. (1986) *Delinquency and Identity: Juvenile Delinquency in an American Chinatown*. New York: Harrow and Heston.

Smith, J., J. Mercy and M. Rosenberg (1986) 'Suicide and Homicide Among Hispanics in the Southwest', *Public Health Reports*, vol. 101, pp. 265-270.

Stiffman, A. and L. Davis (1990) *Ethnic Issues in Adolescent Mental Health*. Newbury Park: Sage Publications.

Tatum, B. (1987) *Assimilation Blues*. New York: Greenwood Press.

Vigil, D. (1988) *Barrio Gangs*. Austin, TX: University of Texas Press.

Wilson, A. (1990) *Black on Black Violence: The Psychodynamics of Black Self-Annihilation in Service of White Domination*. New York: Afrikan World Infosystems.

Wolfstetter-Kausch, H. and E. Gaier (1981) 'Alienation Among Black Adolescents', *Adolescence*, vol. 16(2), pp. 471-485.

Yeakey, C. and C. Bennett (1990) 'Race, Schooling and Class in American Society', *Journal of Negro Education*, vol. 59(1), pp. 3-17.

Young, T. (1989) 'Alienation and Self-Reported Deviance', *Psychological Reports*, vol. 65, pp. 727-730.

Zahar, R. (1974) *Frantz Fanon: Colonialism and Alienation*. New York: Monthly Review Press.

Index

Acosta, E. 36
African American
  class structure 19-21
  economic structure 8-9
  political structure 9-10
  socio-cultural status 10-11
African American church 24-25
African American youths
  and racial inequality 21-22
  social support for 23-25
Agnew, R. 15n, 17
Aguirre, A. 41n
Alianza del las Mercedes 34
alienation
  behavioral adaptations to 6-7, 27
  cultural alienation 6, 56-57, 72, 75
  from general other 6, 56-57, 72, 74
  from racial or social group 6, 56-57, 72-73
  from social praxis 6, 57, 72, 75
  self-alienation 6, 56-57, 71-72
  variants of 18
anomie 3
  See also strain theories
anova findings 67-75
assimilation 6, 63
Austin, R. 14n

Babbie, E. 45
Barrera, M. 29n
Baskin, D. 79

Bean, F. 38
Blauner, R. 27, 53
Burgess, E. 2

class
  measurement of 62-65
classic structural theories 1-4
  comparison with colonial model 11-12
  limitations of 4-5
  See also anomie, delinquent subcultures, opportunity theory and social disorganization theory
Cloward, R. 3-4, 14n, 52
Cohen, A. 3-4, 14n
colonial model 5-8
  comparison with classic structural theories 11-13
  limitations of 16-27
Community Service Organization 34
concentric circle theory 2
Copelin, B. 39
crime 7-8, 58-59
  alcohol use 61-62
  minor delinquency 60, 62
  moderate delinquency 60, 62
  property crime 61-62
  serious delinquency 60, 62
Cullen, F. 17
Curry, E. 79

Denton, N. 38

differential response to shared
   oppression 16-18

Elliott, D. 65n

Fagan, J. 79
Fanon, F. 6-7, 16
Farnworth, M. 58-59, 62
Feagin, J. 32
Fix, M. 38, 41
Frazier, E. 15n

G. I. Forum 34
Genelin, M. 39
general causal model of delinquency
   77-81
Gillis, A. 62
Goedicke, W. 38

Hacker, A. 20, 45
Hagan, J. 62
Harrington, P. 38
Hawkins, D. 22
Hendin, H. 79
Hispanic Americans 31-32
Hochschild, J. 22

internal colonialism
   and African Americans 7-11
   and Mexican Americans 32-35

Jaynes, G. 20
Jones, N. 22

Krohn, M. 58-59, 62

Lizotte, A. 58-59, 62
Long, S. 64n

Massey, D. 38
McIntosh, P. 64n
Menard, S. 65n

Merton, R. 3
methodological issues of
   neocolonial model 42-43
Mexican American
   class structure 35-37
Mexican American youths 37
   effect of colonialism on 39-40
Moore, J. 32, 36
Murguia, E. 38

National Crime Victimization
   Survey 39
National Research Council 79
neocolonial model 29-30
   propositions of 27-28
   theoretical contributions of 28-29
   theoretical promise of 97-98

Obu, J. 33
Ohlin, L. 3-4, 14n, 52
opportunity theory 3-4

Park, R. 2
path analysis
   combined sample 81-82
   race and types of delinquency
      81, 83-86, 88-93
perceived oppression
   economic 53-54, 67-68
   political 53-54, 67-68
   social 53-55, 67, 69
pilot study
   limitations of sample 45-47, 52
   measurement of variables 52-63
   sample and sampling procedure
      44-45
   scale construction 52
Pinderhughes, R. 36
Pinkney, A. 35
protest 7, 29

Quinn, J. 24

racial inequality 21-22
  See also underclass, African
  Americans, Mexican Americans
Rodriquez, N. 41n, 64n
Rodriquez, O. 79
Russell, K. 5

Shaw, C. 2
Simpson, J. 62
Sjostrom, B. 36
Skerry, P. 35
Smith, K. 52
social class
  measurement of 62-63
social disorganization theory 1-2
social support 17-18, 23, 58
  family support 23, 58, 69-70
  organizational support 24-25, 58, 69-70
Sommers, I. 79
Stack, C. 23, 57
Staples, R. 14n
Southwell, P. 18

Spaights, E. 79
Steele, L. 37
strain theories 3-4
Struyk, R. 38
Sum, A. 38

Telles, E. 38
theory of delinquent subcultures
  3-4
Thornberry, T. 58-59, 62
Tienda, M. 38
Turner, J. 41n
Turner, M. 38

underclass 19-20
United Farm Workers Union 34

Valdez, A. 37
Vigil, J. 36-37

Weisburn, D. 79
Williams, R. 20
Wilson, J. 19, 41n

About the Author

Becky Tatum is Assistant Professor of Criminal Justice at Georgia State University. She received her Ph.D. from the School of Criminal Justice at the University at Albany. Dr. Tatum's research interests include the etiology of juvenile violence, alternative perspectives on crime, and the interconnections between race, gender and crime. She currently serves as Executive Counselor of the Minorities and Women Section of the Academy of Criminal Justice Sciences, and Secretary of the Division of People of Color and Crime Section of the American Society of Criminology.